How to Probate an Estate

*A Handbook for Executors
and Administrators*

by
William J. Moody

CASTLE BOOKS
NEW YORK

This edition published by arrangement
with Cornerstone Library

CONTENTS

INTRODUCTION

This is not intended to be a legal tome, but rather a practical or "what to do next" guide for the person who suddenly finds himself executor or administrator of an estate—a singular honor, of course, but also a worrisome one.

It is suggested that the user of this book first skim the entire volume so that he will know where to go back to for what. He should then study each section with some degree of care, to fix the general pattern of estate administration in his mind.

As he proceeds in his duties over a period of months or years, he might then return for more specific information.

There are several sections which contain recommendations to take some action immediately. If there is any doubt about the solvency of the estate, or any possibility of a will contest, these actions should be postponed until the executor knows he can proceed in the usual manner.

It is incumbent upon the writer to warn that this is not intended as a substitute for legal advice. This is intended to help the executor in the performance of his lay duties and also, if this is possible, to help him understand the lawyer of his choice.

PART 1

The Estate
Check List

Every person who acts as executor or administrator of an estate should utilize an estate check list. Such a check list is reproduced below. This check list is designed to indicate all actions which are required, or which may be desired, in the administration of an estate. Some of the items listed may not be necessary in a particular estate, but a determination should be made in each instance as to whether or not they are necessary.

At the outset of the administration, the executor should go through this list with his attorney, determine what steps are required and at what date they should be completed. In a general way, the check list is in chronological order, but there is no hard and fast rule that the steps must be taken in this order. Steps one through thirty-five will usually be completed within the first sixty days. The other items as the law requires, or as events permit. The required times are indicated for Federal Estate Tax matters, but the State requirements will vary by jurisdiction.

When the listed job is completed, the date of completion should be indicated on the list.

Faithful use of the check list will enable the executor to

7

have a running calendar of events, eliminate doubts as to whether he is doing everything he should, and at any given time see the complete picture of what has been accomplished and what remains to be done.

The list below is keyed to sections in this book for forms and further information.

CHECK LIST FOR DECEDENT'S ESTATE

ESTATE OF .... PROBATE NO. ....

ADDRESS .... DATE OF DEATH ....

ATTORNEY .... DATE OF APPT. ....

ACCOUNTANT .... SOC. SEC. NO. ....

CO-EXECUTOR .... TAX I.D. NO. ....

Description of Item   *Date Completed*

1. Discuss probate with the attorney (Hiring the Attorney) ....
2. Probate will and publish notice of probate ....
3. Obtain certified copy of will and certificates of appointment ....
4. Apply for tax identification number ....
5. Publish notice to creditors ....
6. Petition for family allowance or provide cash for family ....
7. Check insurance on property ....
8. File change of address with postmaster ....
9. Search and inventory household, and arrange for storage of valuables ....
10. Determine what to do with automobiles ....
11. Discontinue utilities and charge accounts ....
12. Petition court for authority to continue business ....
13. Check with employer for unpaid salary and any company benefits ....

14. Settle brokerage accounts ....
15. Contact all local banks and savings associations ....
16. Establish fiduciary bank account and invest excess funds ....
17. Inventory safe deposit box ....
18. Notify dividend and interest paying agents or transfer securities ....
19. Determine property passing direct ....
20. Secure information on real estate owned ....
21. Examine personal records and tax returns ....
22. Pay funeral bill and obtain discount ....
23. Determine whether other debts should be paid ....
24. File claims for life and other insurance and obtain IRS Forms 712 ....
25. File for social security, civil service and veterans benefits ....
26. Appraise property and have appraisers appointed ....
27. File inventory and appraisement ....
28. Pay appraisers' fees ....
29. Consider distribution or sale of personal property ....
30. Notify beneficiaries ....
31. File Income Tax Returns ....
32. Determine cash requirements ....
33. Consider monument or headstone ....
34. File Estate Tax Preliminary Notice (2 months) ....
35. Employ ancillary administrator if necessary ....
36. Should widow file election ....
37. Check for claims and establish reserves ....
38. Petition for attorneys' and executors' fees ....
39. File Estate Tax Returns ....

9

1. HIRING THE ATTORNEY:

Every executor* must employ an attorney to represent
him in the probate court. The extent of the attorney's par-
ticipation in the administration of the state, and consequent-
ly the general amount of his fee, will depend upon you as
executor. The quicker the relationship with the attorney is
established, the better.

It is the executor's prerogative to choose his attorney.
As a trust officer, I have a virtually inflexible rule of hiring
the attorney who wrote the will. This has the merit of having someone who is already familiar with the affairs of
the deceased. The same would apply to accountants if they
are required.

You should not hesitate to arrive at an agreement with
the attorney as to his fees. The fees need not be set at a
dollar amount, and most attorneys would be reluctant to so
do. However, an agreement to base his fee upon a fixed
percentage of the probate assets would be equitable, as
would agreement to use Bar Association schedules. A
word of caution in this respect: Do not rely on a cut-rate
lawyer to represent you; the matter is too important and
the potential liability too extensive.

* Throughout this handbook the words "executor" and "administrator" are used interchangeably, where either will do, rather than the
more unwieldy term of "personal representative." See the glossary for
precise meanings of these and other terms.

In order that the arrangement with the attorney can be fair to both parties, a review of the check list set out here, and a decision as to who will do what, should be made. This review will serve to facilitate an agreement with the attorney, and to save the estate money.

2. PROBATE WILL AND PUBLISH NOTICE OF PROBATE:

Actually, to probate a will means to prove the will. The Probate Court is the court having jurisdiction over the proving of wills. In popular connotation, probating a will has become synonymous with administering or settling an estate, from the death of the testator to the distribution to the beneficiaries.

Probating the will is a legal proceeding; therefore, your attorney will prepare and file the necessary papers.

If the will is in your possession, turn it over to the attorney and obtain his receipt, or deliver it to the probate court and obtain a receipt.

The attorney will need to know the names and addresses of the heirs at law, which are, generally speaking, the spouse and nearest of blood kindred. Also the addresses of the beneficiaries of the will. He should also be told if there are any minors.

Whether publication of notice is required will depend on the law of your state, as will the form of publication. Your attorney or the court will handle this.

3. OBTAIN CERTIFIED COPIES OF WILL AND CERTIFICATES OF APPOINTMENT:

A certified copy is one to which a court official attaches a certificate to show that it is a true copy of the one in the court files. Initially you should order one for your file. This is advisable even though there may be carbon copies, so that there can be no doubt that you are working from the correct instrument.

11

A certificate of appointment, also called "letters testamentary" or "letters of administration," is a court document stating that you are the executor or administrator of the estate. Some courts issue short form certificates which will serve most purposes.

You will be required to supply your certificate of appointment to the banks and other companies to obtain possession of the bank accounts or other property. A certificate is usually not acceptable if it is in excess of sixty days old, so you should only order those for which you have immediate need. Subsequent copies may be ordered when needed. Other sections of this handbook will indicate the need for certification for specific purposes.

4. APPLY FOR TAX IDENTIFICATION NUMBER:

Every estate must apply to the Internal Revenue Service for a tax identification number. This number will be used on the Fiduciary Income Tax Returns (Form 1041.) The form is obtained from the IRS office. A sample form is reproduced below with the necessary blanks completed.

5. PUBLISH NOTICE TO CREDITORS:

All jurisdictions have a requirement that a notice be filed to inform creditors of the death, and give them an opportunity to file a claim. The form of publication varies from state to state, as does the time within which creditors must file. Your attorney will know how to proceed.

It is of the utmost importance that the executor make sure that the notice is published. If the notice is not given, distribution cannot be made, or if made, the executor incurs a personal liability for any outstanding claims. Conversely, a creditor is barred if he fails to file within the time limit.

There are procedures for filing objections to claims, and for settlement of disputed claims, which depend on state law, and upon which your attonery can advise you.

12

FOR CLEAR COPY ON ALL PARTS TYPEWRITE OR PRINT WITH BALL POINT PEN—PRESS FIRMLY
(See Instructions on Reverse)

FORM SS-4 (1-65)
PART 1   U.S. TREASURY DEPARTMENT – INTERNAL REVENUE SERVICE
APPLICATION FOR EMPLOYER IDENTIFICATION NUMBER

PLEASE LEAVE BLANK

1. NAME *(TRUE name as distinguished from TRADE name.)*

ESTATE OF JOHN DOE, deceased

2. TRADE NAME, IF ANY *(Enter name under which business is operated, if different from item 1.)*

3. ADDRESS OF PRINCIPAL PLACE OF BUSINESS.*(No. and Street, City, State, Zip Code)*

1011 1st Ave., S., Anycity, N.Y. 10032

4. COUNTY

York

5. CHECK (X) TYPE OF ORGANIZATION *(If "other" specify, such as "Estate," etc.)*

☐ Individual   ☐ Corporation   ☐ Partnership   ☒ Other *(Specify)* Estate

5 a. Ending month of accounting year
Dec.

6. If individual, enter your social security account number

7. REASON FOR APPLYING *(If "other" specify such as "Corporate structure change," "Acquired by gift or trust," etc.)*

☐ Started new business   ☐ Purchased going business   ☒ Other New Estate

8. Date you acquired or started business *(Mo., day, year)*
12/15/68 d/d

9. First date you paid or will pay wages *(Mo., day, year)*
N/A

10. NATURE OF BUSINESS *(See Instructions)*

N/A

11. NUMBER OF EMPLOYEES

	Agricultural	Non-agricultural
	0	0

12. If nature of business is MANUFACTURING, list in order of their importance the principal products manufactured and the estimated percentage of the total value of all products which each represents.

		PLEASE	LEAVE	BLANK
1	%	R	DO	TA
2	% 3	%		
		FR		FRC

13. Do you operate more than one place of business?   ☐ Yes   ☐ No
If "Yes," attach a list showing for each separate establishment:
a. Name and address.   b. Nature of business.   c. Number of employees.

14. To whom do, you sell most of your products or services?

☐ Business establishments   ☐ General public   ☐ Other *(Specify)*

PLEASE LEAVE BLANK

Geo.	Ind.	Class	Size	Reas. for Appl.	Bus. Bir. Date

FORM SS-4 (1-65)
PART 2

DO NOT DETACH ANY PART
OF THIS FORM. SEND ALL COPIES TO
THE DISTRICT DIRECTOR OF INTERNAL REVENUE

PLEASE LEAVE BLANK

NAME AND COMPLETE ADDRESS

1. NAME *(TRUE name as distinguished from TRADE name.)*

ESTATE OF JOHN DOE, deceased

2. TRADE NAME, IF ANY *(Enter name under which business is operated, if different from item 1.)*

3. ADDRESS OF PRINCIPAL PLACE OF BUSINESS *(No. and Street)*

1011 1st Ave., S.

(City, State, Zip Code)

Anycity, N.Y. 10032

4. COUNTY

York

. CHECK (X) TYPE OF ORGANIZATION *(If "other" specify, such as "Estate," etc.)*

☐ Individual   ☐ Corporation   ☐ Partnership   ☒ Other *(Specify)* Estate

5 a. Ending month of accounting year
Dec.

6. If individual, enter your social security account number

7. REASON FOR APPLYING *(If "other" specify such as "Corporate structure change," "Acquired by gift or trust," etc.)*

☐ Started new business   ☐ Purchased going business   ☒ Other New Estate

8. Date you acquired or started business *(Mo., day, year)*
12/15/68 d/d

9. First date you paid or will pay wages *(Mo., day, year)*
N/A

10. NATURE OF BUSINESS *(See Instructions)*

N/A

11. NUMBER OF EMPLOYEES

	Agricultural	Non-agricultural
	0	0

12. Have you ever applied for an identification number for this or any other business?   ☒ No   ☐ Yes
If "Yes," enter name and trade name (if any). Also enter the approximate date, city, and state where you first applied and previous number if known.

DATE
12-26-68

SIGNATURE

TITLE
Executor

13

Occasionally you will find yourself with a creditor who has failed to file his claim within the allotted time period. You are under no obligation to honor such a claim; however, I have found people reluctant to let a legitimate bill go unpaid. In this situation, you should obtain the consent, in writing, of the residuary beneficiaries before paying the debt. A letter from you pointing out that there is no obligation to pay because of the law, but that you feel the claim is justified, and a reply approving the payment, will suffice.

6. PETITION FOR FAMILY ALLOWANCE, ETC.:

The statutes of the various states provide that the courts may order the executor to pay certain amounts for the support of the widow and minor children during the period of administration. Check with the attorney for the exact provision of the statute. If the widow has sufficient funds, it may not be necessary, or even advisable to do this.

In addition, if the estate is obviously solvent, the executor may get additional funds into the hands of the family either by advances or partial distributions; or possibly by creating a trust if such is provided by the will. The executor assumes the risk when be does so, but I have never hesitated where it is necessary, and where the likelihood of insolvency is minimal.

7. CHECK INSURANCE ON PROPERTY:

This is one of the very first things that an executor should do. The executor can be held liable if he permits a policy to lapse, or fails to cover the estate against loss by either casualty or liability.

Check the policies with two things in mind:

    (1)   Is the coverage complete?

    (2)   Is the coverage adequate?

By complete coverage, I mean the extent of the coverage, that is, both real estate and personal property should be covered for fire and extended coverage, which includes theft, storm, etc. Improved real estate should also be insured against liability. Home-owners policies will lapse if the property is no longer used as a residence, so these should be changed.

Items of unique value, such as jewelry, furs, collections of stamps or coins, should be insured by a special policy or a separate schedule to the regular policy.

If deceased was a landlord there should be Owners-Landlords-Tenants (OLT) coverage for liability. If he owned a mortgage there should be an owner's policy with a loss payable to the mortgagee.

There should be a determination as to the adequacy of the coverage. Frequently owners under-insure their property, either being willing to risk some loss, or because increases in value have been ignored. The executor should immediately examine the property and bring the coverage up to par according to his own judgment. After the appraisement has been made, he should again examine the policies and bring them into line with the appraised value.

Advise the insurance companies, as soon as practical, that you are executor and that the policies should be made payable to the estate. Where the policies are on property which passes to a survivor by virtue of joint ownership, advise him to acquire his own insurance, cancel the estate's policy after allowing him a reasonable time to do so, and request a refund of unearned premium. If the joint owner is a family member you may simply want to transfer the policies and forget the unearned premium.

A specific legatee becomes the holder of the title to real estate immediately upon the death of the owner, although subject to the control of the executor during administration. Most attorneys interpret this to mean that the beneficiary becomes liable for such charges as insurance and taxes from the date of death. If this be the case, such party should be charged with these items.

15

Once the insurance has been reviewed and corrected to your satisfaction, set up your calendar or ticklers (reminder file) to make sure that the future premiums are timely paid and endorsements received.

8. CHANGE OF ADDRESS:

Whether to put in a change of address at the post office will depend upon the circumstances. You may not want to do so if there is a member of the family living in the house, but rather advise them to hold the mail for you.

If the party lived alone, or with persons not members of his family, you will request that mail be forwarded to you. Usually a letter to the postmaster, or a change of address card, will do. A form follows:

Postmaster,

Carson City, Fla.

Dear Sir:

The undersigned has been appointed Executor of the Estate of Mary Thin, who lived at 2345 First Street, S.E. Please forward all her mail to me at the above address. A certified copy of my letters is enclosed.

Very truly yours,

You will, of course, want to notify all correspondents as soon as practical.

Occasionally a gift will come in the mail from someone who had not heard of the death. I return such gifts with a note stating our regrets that the party had not been notified. In a similar manner, personal letters and cards can be answered.

In other chapters, there is advice on how to handle other matters, such as credit cards, stock holdings, etc.

9. SEARCH AND INVENTORY THE HOMEPLACE:

Making a search of the residence and an inventory of its

contents can be a tedious chore, or a simple matter. The thoroughness of the search and completeness of the inventory is largely a matter of discretion. The following are in the nature of guidelines. To cover all conceivable situations would result in a volume devoted to this subject alone. Perhaps the first rule should be: when in doubt, be thorough and particular. On the other hand, if circumstances are such that this would be a waste of time, a more practical approach can be used. The following examples may be helpful in making this decision.

When a person lives alone, especially an elderly person, rumors abound that he or she was a miser, and has millions hidden in the mattress. This situation calls for a complete search and extensive records. The form of inventory is set out below:

John Black Estate
Inventory of the Contents of the homeplace at
1234 Fifth Place, S., Clearwater, Florida

Living Room
Sofa and 2 matching chairs
1 wooden rocking chair
Ottoman
2 floor lamps
1 table lamp
1 Oil Painting by C. Shultz
2 pictures (reproductions)
1 5' x 7' wall mirror
3 throw rugs

Dining Room
Dining Room Suite consisting of table & 6 chairs, sideboard, china cabinet.
Set of dishes, 8 each plates, cups, saucers, dessert plates, 1 gravy boat, 1 bowl.
8 Crystal goblets.
Miscellaneous dishes and linens.

Sterling service for eight (six pieces each).
9' x 12' rug.

Kitchen
Westinghouse refrigerator
General Electric Stove
China cupboard
Dishes, pots, pans and various utensils

Bedroom
Bedroom Suite consisting of bed, end table, dressing
table, chest of drawers.
6 throw rugs
2 chairs
1 table lamp

Garage
"Snapping Turtle" power lawn mower—24".
Miscellaneous hand tools
Wheelbarrow
Miscellaneous yard tools
50' garden hose

The undersigned hereby certify that the foregoing is a
true and complete inventory of the house at 1234 5th Place
South, made on the 28th of December, 1968.

_____

_____

The opposite situation occurs when a man lived with
his wife and she is his principal beneficiary. Here only
those items of unusual nature or particular value need be
listed: such things as jewelry, paintings and first editions.
Ordinary household furnishings and personal effects can
be listed just that way, e.g., Six rooms of household furniture . . . . . $2,000.
Although it may be expedient to take the shortcut indi-

cated above, it should be kept in mind that there may be collateral benefits to making the inventory complete, for example, in the event of an insurance claim. I suppose the moral is that you can't go wrong if you do it right.

10. DETERMINE WHAT TO DO WITH AUTOMOBILES:

On the surface, this appears to be a matter of minor importance, but it can also be troublesome and subject the executor to criticism. Keep in mind that an automobile is a rapidly depreciating asset, and, even worse, is a dangerous animal. More lawsuits arise out of traffic accidents than any other single cause, and the estate could be subject to liability.

The first thing to do is to make sure that there is adequate insurance coverage ... liability, collision and comprehensive.

If the car is left to a member of the family, it is very difficult to tell them they can't drive it, so the best thing to do is transfer the title as soon as possible.

If the car is left to someone other than a member of the immediate family, put the car in storage until it is appraised and then transfer it to the proper party. Again, this should be done as soon as possible, unless there is some doubt about the solvency of the estate, or a possibility that the will might be contested.

If the car is a part of the general estate, and is to be sold, sell it as soon as possible. First, obtain one or more appraisals, preferably obtaining both the retail and wholesale prices. If there is no authority given in the will to sell assets, obtain court approval for a public sale.

If you have the power of sale in the will, you may sell at public or private sale. My preference is to obtain at least three sealed bids, but in some cases this is not possible, so sell it for the best deal you can make. In the case of cars, there is ample justification for the quick sale, rather than trying to hold out for the last dollar.

11. DISCONTINUE UTILITIES AND CHARGE ACCOUNTS:

I think it fairly obvious that this should be done. The only question is when and how.

Certainly if keeping the lights, water, etc., on is for the preservation or safety of the property, the executor can do so, and pay the expenses from estate funds. If not, they should be discontinued as soon as the executor has made his search and the appraisers have done their work.

If the family is continuing residence in the house, then as soon as can be done diplomatically, the accounts with the utility companies should be transferred to the survivor.

Charge accounts should be cancelled immediately. I have known some people to merely destroy the charge cards; however, I prefer to send the cards back to the issuing company with a letter cancelling the account and requesting an acknowledgment.

If a widow wishes to continue the account, ask that a new account be established in her name and new cards issued.

If you are reasonably confident that the estate is solvent, the bills can be paid immediately without asking that a claim be filed. There is additional comment on the payment of bills in Section 37.

12. PETITION COURT FOR AUTHORITY TO CONTINUE BUSINESS:

There are three primary types of business enterprises: the sole proprietorship, the partnership and the corporation. In this section we are coupling the closely held, or family corporation, with the other two, as the inherent problems are similar. The closely held corporation is one in which the deceased was the controlling stockholder, or pernaps the sole stockholder, and the moving force behind the operation.

In a proprietorship, the Estate becomes the owner of

the assets of the business and responsible for the debts. A partnership under general rules of law terminates upon the death of a partner, with the surviving partner having authority to wind up the business. A corporation continues as a separate entity, with the Estate becoming the controlling stockholder.

As time may be of the essence, the Executor should act as quickly as possible. The following steps are recommended as important to insure against a rapid decline in the value of the business as a going enterprise, and to guard against potential liability:

(1) Examine the will and see if special provisions are made to give the executor authority to continue the operation; if not, obtain a court order to do so.

(2) Determine if there are any partnership purchase or stock purchase agreements extant.

(3) Call a meeting of the officers and employees to explain the situation, asking them to bear with you and telling them that they will be informed of any impending changes.

(4) See that employees are properly bonded.

(5) Appoint a person to take charge of the day to day operation.

(6) Arrange for an immediate audit of the books by an independent Certified Public Accountant.

(7) If the internal controls are inadequate, change the business accounts so that you must countersign the checks.

It is quite common that, where one man is the most important factor in a business, it will rapidly decline in his absence. It is usually best to sell or liquidate as soon as possible. An operating business will usually bring more than a dormant one, so if at all feasible, the business should be kept open pending a sale.

13. CHECK WITH EMPLOYER FOR UNPAID SALARY AND ANY COMPANY BENEFITS:

The employer of the deceased should be contacted to determine if there is any unpaid salary, vacation pay or other benefits. He should be asked about pension or profit sharing benefits, group life or health plans and possibly labor union plans. If any payments are due to the estate, he should be supplied with letters testamentary.

There are special tax rules governing employee benefit plans which should be reviewed by the executor or the named beneficiary before deciding how to take payment from a pension or profit sharing trust.

Payments received from an employee trust are taxed as income; however, if the total amount payable is received in one taxable year of the payee by reason of the death of the employee, the proceeds can be treated as a long term capital gain.

Payments from a pension or profit sharing trust are includable in the taxable estate of the decedent if payable to the estate, but are not if payable to a named beneficiary or to a trust which was established during decedent's lifetime. In any event, the executor will be required to list the data concerning such payments on the estate tax return, and should obtain the necessary information. See the sample return in Section 39.

Insurance claims are covered in Section 24.

There is also an exclusion from gross income of the beneficiaries of the estate of a deceased employee of up to $5,000 of death benefits paid by or for the employer. Your attorney or accountant should be asked to check this point when the tax return is done.

This exclusion does not rule out the possibilities that payments to a widow of an employee by the employer may be gifts, and thus not taxable as income. There has been considerable litigation on this subject, so the facts should be carefully examined before a decision is made.

14. SETTLE BROKERAGE ACCOUNTS:

Two main types of brokerage accounts will be considered. Of course all accounts should be examined, and verified. If there is evidence of an account, such as a statement from a broker, no matter how old, that firm should be contacted to see if there are any current transactions pending.

Margin accounts, that is, those accounts in which the broker is holding securities as collateral, should be liquidated as soon as practical. The executor has no authority to deal on margin under ordinary circumstances, and should be chary of doing so even when given broad powers in the will.

Open accounts should be either closed or transferred to the estate. A copy of the appointment should be supplied to the broker. The executor should take possession of any securities in the hands of the broker. All pending buy and sell orders should be cancelled until the executor gets familiar with the estate situation.

15. CONTACT ALL BANKS AND SAVINGS AND LOAN ASSOCIATIONS:

This may well become cumbersome in metropolitan areas, so the executor will have to use his own judgment as to which to contact. Remember, though, that it is better to contact too many than not enough. I always contact the local banks and savings associations, and any out of town if there is any evidence that the decedent may have done business with them. A sample letter follows:

April 29, 1970

Second National Bank,
Anytown, USA
Re: Estate of Hubert Hub

Gentlemen:

The undersigned has qualified as Executor of the Estate of Hubert Hub, deceased, who lived at 23

Holly St., This City. Will you please let me know if he had a checking account, savings account, safe deposit box, or was doing any other business with your institution.

I will supply a certified copy of my letters testamentary upon request.

Very truly yours,

You will want to close out all demand accounts (checking) and bring all cash together in your fiduciary account (Section 16,) but it is advisable to leave savings until the next interest paying period. Subsequent to that, no account should exceed the insured limits. If you have excess cash on hand, have your bank purchase United States Treasury Bills for you.

16. ESTABLISH FIDUCIARY BANK ACCOUNT AND INVEST EXCESS FUNDS:

There is an absolute prohibition against a fiduciary (executor, administrator, guardian or trustee) mixing funds of the estate with his own. Such commingling is almost tantamount to embezzlement, and any doubts would be resolved in favor of the estate. Likewise, an executor could be discharged without compensation for so doing.

Your bank will help you establish a separate account in the name of the estate, and imprint checks as follows:

Estate of John Blank, deceased

by ....

Executor

All funds coming into the hands of the executor should be deposited to this account, and all payments on behalf of the estate should be by check from this account. Should an advance of cash be unavoidable, a receipt should be obtained so that when the executor reimburses himself he can show justification.

24

An accurate accounting should be kept by separate ledger, with all transactions being fully described.

One of the primary criticisms of individuals who act as executors is their failure to invest excess cash during the period of administration. Any cash not required for immediate needs should be put to work.

The executor, of course, cannot speculate with estate funds. He does, however, have several sources of investment which are not speculative.

He can utilize savings accounts in banks and savings and loan associations, keeping any given account within the insured limits. He might also use certificates of deposit, if he can accurately judge his time element.

Probably his best bet is United States Treasury Bills. Bills can be bought through his local bank for periods of thirty days to one year, and will give him a respectable return regardless of when he needs the money and must sell them. They are bought at a discount in units of $1,000 or more.

17.   INVENTORY THE SAFE DEPOSIT BOX:

How one proceeds to inventory the lock box depends largely on the state in which you live.

If you live in a state which has an inheritance tax which exceeds the federal tax credit, in all probability the procedures are established by law, and your attorney will have to coordinate your plans with the taxing authorities.

If you live in a state which does not require that the box be sealed, you will, as executor, be the one to enter the box. The bank or safe deposit box company will require that you have a certified copy of your letters testamentary. You, or your attorney, obtain this from the court.

How you proceed from here is largely a discretionary matter. I have found the following to be effective and efficient.

First of all, it is advisable to invite a member of the

family who is a primary beneficiary to be present, provided one is readily available. I also invite the attorney; I also take along one of my staff. Never enter a box alone.

Those present are advised that they will be asked to certify an inventory of the box. The box should then be opened, and the contents sorted into various classifications, and listed with as complete a description as practical. The following is a suggested format:

CONTENTS OF LOCK BOX #436, FIRST NATIONAL BANK OF BLACKVILLE

Cash in the amount of $23.00

Coins as follows:

$	2.35	in nickels
	10.00	gold coin—U. S.
	1.00	Mexican
	3.98	Indian Head pennies

First National Bank Savings Passbook #3456 showing a balance of $7,898 as of 7-5-68.

Bonds:

$ 300.00 U. S. Series E Bonds reg John H. Smith with P.O.D. Mary Smith

No. 2345678E due 9-78 @ 100
No. 8765432E due 4-69 @ 200

5,000.00 U. S. Treas. Bd., 4%, due 6-15-92 with SCA (this means subsequent coupons attached)

Stocks:

100 Shs General Motors Corp. com reg John H. Smith
Ctf. No. 345 @ 75
Ctf. No. 432 @ 25

Deeds:

Warranty deed from James Jones to John H. Smith and Mary Smith, JTWRS, covering property in the N ½ of the NW ¼ Sec 3 T 4 E, R 3 W, Flatt County, Florida, containing about 6 acres, recorded Page 56, Book 567.

(For the purposes of the inventory, real estate descriptions can be brief so long as they are adequate, to differentiate the deed from others. The recording information also does this.)

Notes and Mortgages:

$ 400.00   Note of Frank Hill dated 6-7-57, 6%, due 9-1-70, unsecured, showing a balance due of $120.00

5000.00   Note of Jane Hill dated 6-7-57, 5%, payable $50 monthly, secured by mortgage on Lot 1, Blk 4, Pleasant Hills Sub., Blackville.

Miscellaneous papers of no apparent value.

The undersigned hereby certify that 'the foregoing is a complete, true and correct inventory of the Safe Deposit Box described above, which was opened in their presence on the 7th day of August, 1979.

_____

(All should sign)

If the list is typed, it of course becomes your permanent record. There is no reason why a handwritten list could not be signed and serve the same purpose. A handy device to use is a dictating machine, in which case the parties should orally certify the tape, and the tape should be saved until they have signed the typed copy, so that they could listen to it if they had any doubts; or, as another approach, the box could be resealed until the inventory is typed and then the contents checked against the typed copy.

The importance of care in the preparation of this inventory cannot be over-emphasized. Both cash and negotiable securities, as well as jewelry, are most often deposited in the box, and failure to be able to support the list could prove somewhat embarrassing.

27

18. NOTIFY DIVIDEND AND INTEREST PAYING AGENTS:

Even though a change of address may have been sent to the post office, it is advisable to have the checks for dividends on stocks, interest on registered bonds and related correspondence sent directly to the executor. It should not be necessary to change the registration to the name of the estate, as the checks can be deposited to the estate account. Ultimately the securities will have to be either sold or transferred to the recipients, and it is unnecessary work to make two transfers. Of course, if the bank or company refuses to permit you to deposit the checks you will have to make the transfer. There is no reason why they should, and I have seldom encountered this situation.

The large corporations either maintain a stock transfer office, a professional transfer agent, or a bank to handle the transfer of their stocks and bonds, and to pay the dividends and interest. Banks and brokers have books which will tell you the name and address of the stock transfer agents and the dividend or interest paying agent. If no such service is available to you, write either the company office or the transfer agent whose name appears on the stock certificate. The following is a proposed letter:

Morris Bank & Trust Company

Wall Street

New York, N. Y.

                        Re: General A Co. common stock

Gentlemen:

The undersigned has been appointed Executor of the Estate of Harry Hud, deceased, who lived at One Main St., Irving, Vermont. I have found 100 shares of General A Co. common stock registered in his name.

Please verify the extent of his holdings, and mark your

records to send all dividends and other correspondence relating to said stock to the undersigned.

Very truly yours,

Occasionally there will be no record in any of the services of a company's existence. If this be the situation, write the Secretary of State of the state of incorporation and ask for information as to the corporate existence and its location. The name of the state of incorporation appears on the stock certificate.

When the time comes to transfer securities to the names of the beneficiaries, endorse the certificates as executor of the estate, and send them to the transfer agent together with a copy of your letters of appointment, certified within sixty days. The transfer agent will advise you if it has further requirements. If there are several certificates for one company, you may use an "Assignment Separate from Certificate," also called a "stock power."

19. DETERMINE PROPERTY PASSING DIRECT:

There will nearly always be property which passes directly from the decedent to another party without reference to the will, and over which the executor has no control. This property passes by reason of the method of holding title, by contract or by law. Some examples are:

(1) Jointly held property. Property, either real estate, securities or bank accounts may be held as joint tenants with right of survivorship. This property passes directly to the survivor, but may, however, be subject to estate or inheritance tax.

(2) By contract. Insurance policies are a contractual relationship between the insured and the owner of the policy, and the proceeds are payable directly to the named beneficiaries.

(3) Various types of trusts. There are certain types of trusts which may be established by a person by

naming themselves as trustee, and over which they exercise complete control during their lifetime, but which become the property of the beneficiary upon their death.

Even though this type of property will never be part of the estate, the executor may have certain duties with respect to it.

First, he will have to determine if the property is subject to estate taxes. Any property which the decedent owned or enjoyed the benefits of will be taxable in his estate. The executor will, therefore, have to determine the value for tax purposes.

If there is property for which the decedent was acting in a fiduciary capacity, i.e., executor, trustee or custodian, the executor of his estate will have to manage or preserve the property until either a new fiduciary is appointed or delivery can be made to the proper party.

20. SECURE INFORMATION ON REAL ESTATE OWNED:

The first thing to do, of course, is to find out what real estate decedent owned. Aside from examining his own record, the local tax assessor's records may be helpful. If in doubt after doing these things, you may want to have a title company make a search for you. This latter is expensive, but if there is doubt it should be pursued.

Next, it should be determined how the title is held. The most frequent methods of holding title other than in one's own name alone are as follows:

(1) Joint Tenants with Right of Survivorship with one or more other persons. This property passes to the survivor.

(2) Tenants in Common. This is when two or more parties hold title without words of survivorship. The undivided interest becomes estate property; for example, if there are two tenants in common,

30

each owns an undivided one-half of the whole, and half of the value is in the estate.

(3) Tenants by the Entirety. This is a style of ownership which can only exist between husband and wife, and the surviving spouse becomes the owner of the whole. Some states have abolished this type.

(4) Homestead. Some states provide for a life estate for the widow, with the children becoming the owner upon her death. This is limited to the residence or farm with certain limitations as to size.

In all situations the property should be examined by the executor and appraised for the estate tax return.

If the property is rented or leased, the tenant should be notified as to whom the rent should be paid.

21. EXAMINE PERSONAL RECORDS AND TAX RETURNS:

The executor must become intimately familiar with the business of the decedent, and the way to do this is to make an exhaustive study of his personal papers.

Copies of past income tax returns will give information about his financial status by revealing his sources of income, and such items as depreciation schedules on rental property. It might also lead to discovery of assets not otherwise known; for example, where stocks are being held by a broker or mutual fund company. If no returns are found, copies can be obtained from the Internal Revenue Service by the payment of a small fee.

The question frequently arises as to what to destroy and what to keep. During the initial examination of the papers, they can be sorted into those which may require further action and those which are apparently worthless. The worthless papers can then be kept until the executor is discharged by the court, and either turned over to the family or destroyed.

There may be occasions when you do not want to reveal

information coming into your possession, such as that when I found a miscellaneous assortment of local hotel keys and chose not to mention them.

22. PAY FUNERAL BILL AND OBTAIN DISCOUNT:

The funeral bill, like any other bill, is a debt for which a claim must be filed, and the executor need not pay it until the claim period expires. However, it might be possible to obtain a discount by paying the bill promptly. By statute, the funeral bill, up to a stipulated amount, is a preferred claim. This must be taken into consideration in an insolvent estate.

23. DETERMINE WHETHER OTHER DEBTS SHOULD BE PAID:

There is considerable difference of opinion among authorities as to whether debts should be paid before the creditors' period expires. There is, of course, no requirement that they be paid before this claim period has passed. I have never seen any reason to wait unless there is a doubt about the solvency of the estate.

A word might be said here about preference of claims and debts. The various states have statutes which set forth the order for payment of debts and expenses. Under these statutes attorneys' and executors' fees and cost of administration have high priority. Likewise do expenses of last illness and, within limits, funeral expenses. Of course, the particular statute must be checked for the exact order of priority.

24. FILE CLAIMS FOR LIFE AND OTHER INSURANCE:

If the life insurance is payable to the estate of the deceased, or to the "executors or administrators of the estate," or if there is no named beneficiary or the named beneficiary is deceased, then the executor must file the claims.

First write the insurance company, or contact the local agent, and ask them to verify the beneficiary designation and supply you with claim forms.

When you receive the claim forms, complete them and return them to the insurance company together with a certified copy of the death certificate and a copy of your letters testamentary. At the same time request the insurance company to supply you with Internal Revenue Service Form 712, "Life Insurance Statement." You will need this to file with the estate tax return.

If an individual is named as beneficiary you may want to assist him. In this situation a death certificate is all that will be required. In any event, the executor will need IRS Form 712 referred to above.

Up to this point we have been discussing policies of which the deceased was the owner and the insured. There are two other possibilities. The insured may not have been the owner, in which case the proceeds will not be includable in his estate for tax purposes. There are special rules to cover those cases in which the deceased did not own the policies but paid the premiums. The attorney or C.P.A. should be consulted.

The other situation is when the deceased was the owner of a policy on the life of another. The replacement value of the policy will be includable in the tax of deceased. This figure must be obtained from the insurance company, as it is not necessarily the same as the cash value. Ask the insurance company for Internal Revenue Service Form 938, Life Insurance Statement.

The type of policy referred to above will usually have a provision for the transfer of ownership to persons designated in the policy. For example, the beneficiary may become the owner. If there is no such provision, and the policy is not specifically bequeathed by the will, it becomes a part of the residue of the estate.

If a policy was assigned as security for a debt, the creditor will of course be paid, in which case the named beneficiary may have a claim against the estate for that portion of the proceeds.

In addition to life insurance proceeds the executor should check for accident and hospitalization benefits, fraternal organization and medicare benefits.

25. SOCIAL SECURITY, CIVIL SERVICE AND VETERANS' BENEFITS:

It would be impractical to attempt to delineate the various benefits available to survivors under the various Federal and State Laws. The Veterans Administration or one of the veterans' organizations can help in their areas. There is a social security office in nearly every community in the country, and if the deceased was a civil servant his employer can be contacted to determine his benefits.

Generally speaking, there are benefits available to surviving spouses and minor children from one or more of the several sources named above. In the case of social security and civil service payments, the benefits may extend beyond the age of eighteen for a full time college student.

The social security laws provide a lump sum death benefit. If there is a surviving spouse, he or she must file the application. A death certificate and a marriage certificate are required. If there is no surviving spouse, the executor or administrator files the application, along with a death certificate and a certified copy of his letters. Some offices permit filing by mail, others will require that the applicant appear in person. I usually file by mail and see what happens, in the hope that I can avoid sitting around their offices.

If deceased was a member of a fraternal organization, there may be benefits due from that source. The local secretary can supply this information.

Applying for insurance proceeds, although akin to this, is covered in another section.

26. HAVE APPRAISERS APPOINTED:

The methods by which appraisers are selected fall into three broad categories, all of which will be covered below. The executor will have to discover into which category his jurisdiction falls, and act accordingly.

If the court reserves unto itself the right to appoint the appraisers, the executor will have to work as best he can with them.

If the executor or his attorney is permitted to suggest persons to be appraisers, then he should select them with care. First of all, it is best to obtain the services of a competent appraiser with proper qualifications and good reputation. Even though the Internal Revenue agent may dispute the values, the good appraiser will be prepared to support his position.

The ideal situation is that in which the executor chooses the appraisers himself, and only to appraise that property which must be appraised. If possible, the executor should choose different experts for different items. Obviously, it is better to have a numismatist appraise coins than to have a realtor do it.

Considerable fees can be saved if the executor arrives at values himself, where no expert opinion is needed. The best example of this is securities listed on a stock exchange.

The Estate Tax Return sets out the rules for determining values. In the case of stocks and bonds, the mean between the highest and lowest selling prices is considered the fair market value. These quotations are found in the newspaper, or can be obtained from a stockbroker. The mean is determined as follows:

$$
\begin{array}{llll}
\text{High} & 17\ 1/8 & = & 17.125 \\
\text{Low} & 16\ 5/8 & = & 16.625 \\
& & & 33.750
\end{array}
$$

$$16.875$$
$$2\ /\ 33.75$$

So the mean is 16.875 or 16 7/8, which is the fair market value to be used on the tax return.

There is always discussion as to whether a high or low appraisal should be obtained. The Internal Revenue Code requires that property be appraised at its fair market value, which is defined as what a willing buyer will pay a willing seller for the property. There are many things dependent upon the appraisal. If the property is subsequently sold, the estate tax value becomes the cost basis for capital gain. It may also be the basis for distributing to multiple beneficiaries. It may be the guideline for determining sales price. Taking all into consideration, the appraisers should be told to arrive at the "fair market value" according to their best judgment, and not try to outsmart the service.

27. FILE INVENTORY AND APPRAISEMENT:

Within a stipulated time after your appointment, usually sixty days, you will be required to file an inventory of the estate with the probate court. If your court requires appraisal of all of the assets, this may be combined with the appraisement by having the appraisers approve and sign the inventory. When preparing the inventory, you should keep in mind the information needed for the Estate Tax Return. By compiling this information at this time, a great deal of work will be saved later. Use the fair market value as of the date of death, as described in the instructions to Form 706. Forms can be obtained from your court, or your attorney, for the heading and the verification. The following format should be acceptable by all courts:

INVENTORY AND APPRAISEMENT

Description	*Value 12-17-68*
CASH ON HAND AND IN BANKS:	
Cash on person of decedent	$ 26.52
Balance in checking account No. 3465 First National Bank	2,302.16

36

Savings account No. 6348 First Natl Bank 1,500.00
Certificate of Deposit No. 123 First State Bank 5,000.00

Total $ 8,828.68

BONDS:

$10,000 U.S.Treasury 4% due June 15, 1989
@ 90 $ 9,000.00
Accrued interest to 12-17-68 2.18
$5,000 U.S.Savings Bonds Series H 4.15%
due Aug. 1, 1970 @ 1,000 5,000.00

Total $ 14,002.18

STOCKS:

100 shs American Tel & Tel Co. com @ 51 $ 5,100.00
100 shs Allied Chemical Corp. com @ 32 3,200.00
100 shs Duquesne Light Co. com @ 34 3,400.00
200 shs International Business Machines Co.
com @ 360 72,000.00
100 shs Xerox Corp. com @ 265½ 26,550.00

Total $110,250.00

Real Estate:

House and Lot, 15 Beach Drive, Clearwater,
Fla. described as Lots 12 and 13, New Sub,
recorded in Book 157 Pp 55-56. Single family
dwelling used as homeplace—appraised at $ 37,500.00

Notes and Mortgages:

Note of John G. Bond in original amount of
$4,000 secured by mortgage on Lot 26, New
Sub to Clearwater recorded in Book 163 P 12.
Payable $100 per month @ 6% interest com-
puted monthly. Balance due $ 3,200.00

Sundry Items:

1966 Buick Automobile $ 1,700.00
Man's wrist watch 45.00
Man's diamond ring-1½ carat 1,350.00

Total $ 3,095.00

RECAPITULATION

Cash on hand and in Banks	$ 8,828.68
Bonds	14,002.18
Stocks	110,250.00
Real Estate	37,500.00
Notes and Mortgages	3,200.00
Sundry Items	3,095.00
TOTAL ESTATE	**$176,875.86**

The original of the inventory should be filed with the court, unless this requirement is waived by the will. Copies should be given to the attorney and all of the residuary beneficiaries.

Some professional executors include in the inventory property which passes by operation of law or contract, and is not subject to probate, for example, property held as joint tenants with right of survivorship. I have no violent objection to doing so, but I see no reason to make this a matter of public record where such is not required.

Great care should be used in the preparation of the inventory, as the executor will be required to account for each item appearing therein.

28. PAY APPRAISERS' FEES:

The method by which appraisers' fees are determined will depend upon local statute and custom. Ask your attorney or the probate judge how this is done and act accordingly.

If the executor has the privilege of choosing his own appraisers, he may also be able to negotiate the fees, but generally, these charges are pretty well established.

Once the work is completed to your satisfaction, there is no reason why you should not pay the fees immediately.

29. CONSIDER DISTRIBUTION OF TANGIBLE PERSONAL PROPERTY:

By tangible personal property we mean such items as

furniture, silver and china, jewelry and furs, automobiles and the like, as contrasted to intangible personal property such as stocks and bonds.

If there is a will, these items may be the subject of specific bequests, and if not, they are a part of the residuary estate. If the estate is solvent, there is no reason why these items cannot be distributed immediately, and recepits taken for them.

If they become a part of the residue and there is but one beneficiary the foregoing paragraph is applicable. If there is more than one beneficiary, then you will have to either obtain their agreement on who is to get which items, or sell them and hold the cash as part of the estate. If there is a power of sale in the will you can sell at private sale. If not, you will have to sell at public auction or obtain a court order to sell at private sale.

It is possible to sell or deliver to the beneficiaries of the residue and deduct the appraised value from their shares. However, this is awkward in practice, and I would not want to do so without agreement among the beneficiaries.

Although the executor has the right to retain the tangible personal property until the estate is settled, I have found that it saves time and money to dispose of it as soon as it can safely be done.

30.   NOTIFYING THE BENEFICIARIES:

There may be a legal requirement in your state that the beneficiaries are to be given notice. In that case, of course you will comply. Whether or not there is such a notice, the executor should notify the beneficiaries as soon as possible, with the caution to them not to expect their bequest until such and such a time. In short, determine when distribution can be made, give yourself a margin for procrastination, and you will not be unduly harassed by impatient beneficiaries. This early contact will help you to establish a friendly relationship with them, and make your job a bit easier.

There are, in general, three ways to give this notice:

First: By a formal reading of the will

Second: By informal personal conversation

Third: By post.

A formal reading of the will is a rarity these days, but on occasion can be a useful tool. If members of the family are gathered together, and someone is left out or might be disappointed with his share, reading the will may avoid embarrassment to you. If the will is read in this fashion, we invite the family to the office, or the attorney's office, and one of us or the attorney reads it to them. You might run into a situation where the reading is desired or requested in which case you should comply as outlined above.

If a formal reading is not necessary, for example where everything is left to the wife, or equally to the children, they can be called together and simply told that fact, and given a copy. At this time the opportunity should be used to explain the time elements and the reasons for them. For example, the possible advantage of using year after death values on the estate tax return. The procedures should be outlined in brief. Both of these techniques make the delays more palatable, and may avoid the criticisms so often heard that estates are delayed to build up fees.

If there are out-of-town beneficiaries, charities or corporations, or strangers to the family, they can be notified by mail. These may be divided into two categories: those receiving specific gifts, e.g. 100 shares of A.T. & T. stock; and those who receive a share of the residue. The latter should be supplied with a copy of the will, and ultimately a copy of the inventory and appraisal, as they are entitled to know who gets how much of what. Those receiving specific gifts need only be so advised. Suggested forms for letters follow:

LETTER FOR SPECIFIC GIFTS

Dear Mrs. Smith:

The undersigned is acting as executor of the Estate of Mary Jonas, who died December 5, 1972. We wish to inform you that you have been named as a beneficiary in her will. The pertinent paragraph of the will reads as follows:

"Item 111. I give to my dear friend, Alice Smith, of Rome, Georgia, the sum of Five Thousand Dollars ($5,000.)"

We should be able to make distribution in about twelve months, but will do so sooner if legally possible.

Very truly yours,

Occasionally such a beneficiary, or someone who has no interest, will request a copy of the will. I see no reason to give them one at estate expense, so I advise them that they can get one by contacting the Court and paying the charge.

LETTER TO RESIDUARY BENEFICIARY

Dear Mr. Luckie:

The undersigned is acting as executor of the Estate of Margaret Rich, who died December 22, 1974. This is to advise you that you have been named as a beneficiary under her will, a copy of which is enclosed herewith.

I will be filing an inventory of the Estate within sixty days, and will send you a copy. As this estate is subject to Federal Estate tax, and we have the privilege of electing an alternate valuation date of one year after the date of death, the Estate will not be settled for approximately twenty-five to thirty-seven months. I will keep you informed as to the progress, and should you have any questions, do not hesitate to call me.

Very truly yours,

You will note that in all cases an attempt is made to give essential information, without being overly verbose or technical. An attempt is also made to neutralize the inevitable delays, and also to point out that the beneficiary may profit by waiting.

One final note on notices—check with the attorney as to whether they should be sent by registered mail with return receipt requested. Some states have peculiarities, for example, Florida requires notification to charitable organizations by such method.

I find it quite helpful to have the beneficiaries, personal or corporate, complete a data card for future reference. Forms for such cards are reproduced on facing page.

31.   FILE INCOME TAX RETURNS:

It is the duty of the executor to file income tax returns for the decedent and for the estate. The return for the decedent will be the usual Form 1040, including all income up to the date of death. If there is a surviving spouse, a joint return may be filed, including the decedent's income to the date of death, and the spouse's income for the entire year.

Subsequent to filing decedent's final Form 1040, the estate must file the Fiduciary Income Tax Return, Form 1041. The executor may elect to file this on a fiscal year basis, or file for the remainder of the year of death, and for subsequent calendar years.

There are certain deductions which may be taken on either the Estate Tax Return or on the Income Tax Return. The regulations allow a deduction of reasonable amounts paid or incurred as expenses of administration, including executors' commissions and certain attorneys' fees. Whether to take these deductions on the Estate Tax Return or the Income Tax Return will depend upon the tax bracket of each. If they are taken as income tax deductions, the estate

BENEFICIARY DATA CARD - CORPORATION

CORRECT NAME OF CORPORATION_____

CORRECT ADDRESS_____

TAX I.D. #_____

NAMES OF PRINCIPAL OFFICERS_____

_____

_____

_____

DATE NOTIFICATION RECEIVED_____

      SIGNED_____

          Please complete and return

BENEFICIARY DATA CARD

FULL NAME_____

ADDRESS_____

SOCIAL SECURITY NO._____

DATE OF BIRTH_____

      SIGNATURE _____

DATE NOTIFICATION RECEIVED_____

RELATIONSHIP TO DECEDENT_____

        Please complete and return

must file a statement (in duplicate) that they are not taken as estate tax deductions, and that the right to do so is waived. Where such a situation is indicated, a close study of the instructions, or consultation with your accountant, is advised.

32. DETERMINE CASH REQUIREMENTS:

As soon as the inventory and appraisement is filed, the executor should be able to determine how much cash he is going to need to settle the tax liabilities, pay the expenses and satisfy the specific cash bequests. As soon as the cash needs are determined, the executor should begin to raise the cash. He should not speculate with estate assets. The following is a simple form for determining cash needs:

CASH REQUIREMENTS

Estate of John Smith

Estimated Gross Estate		$410,000
Specific cash bequests	$50,000	
Expenses	28,000	
Debts	20,000	
Estate Taxes	33,000	
	———	
Total cash needed		$131,000
Less:		
Cash on hand	45,000	
Anticipated Income	20,000	
	———	
Total		$ 65,000
		———
Cash to be raised		$ 66,000

33. CONSIDER MONUMENT OR HEADSTONE:

Frequently there will be language in the will directing the executor to erect a "suitable monument or headstone." Of course, he should do so, keeping in mind that the amount spent should be reasonable.

In the absence of such a direction in the will, there is some question as to whether this is a proper charge against estate assets. Even if it is not, there are very few people who would object, and I doubt if anyone would have the gall to raise the question in court if the amount spent was within reason, so as a practical matter I say to use your own judgment, and not worry about the legalities.

34. FILE ESTATE TAX PRELIMINARY NOTICE:

Within two months after the executor qualifies, he must file Internal Revenue Service Form 704,* Estate Tax Preliminary Notice. The primary purpose of this form is to advise the Service that the estate is subject to federal estate tax. This is required for estates of citizens or residents which exceed $60,000 in value. Some professional executors merely indicate on the form that the estate exceeds $60,000. A sample completed form is reproduced on the following pages. Note that the form calls for "approximate" values, so round figures may be used.

35. EMPLOY ANCILLARY ADMINISTRATOR, IF NECESSARY:

In the event that the decedent owned real estate in a state other than his place of residence, it will be necessary to have an administration in that state. Whether or not the domiciliary administrator will be able to act in the foreign state will depend upon the laws of that state.

Your attorney can check the law digest to determine your eligibility to act in the other state. He can also check the legal directory, and contact an attorney to handle the ancillary administration.

*See pages 46 and 47.

FORM 704
U.S. TREASURY DEPARTMENT
INTERNAL REVENUE SERVICE
(Revised Mar. 1963)

ESTATE TAX
PRELIMINARY NOTICE

ESTATE OF CITIZEN OR RESIDENT OF THE
UNITED STATES

(To be executed and filed by executor or person in possession
of property—observe instructions on reverse side)

(Space for use of director)
RECEIVED

Name of decedent .... John J. Smith
Date of death ..December 10, 1968.............. Citizenship (nationality) United States
Place of death ..Clearwater Rest Home, Clearwater, Florida
Residence (domicile) at time of death ..35 Beach Drive, Clearwater, Florida 33501
..................February 5,............., 19.69.

DISTRICT DIRECTOR OF INTERNAL REVENUE, (*Nonresident citizens see instructions*)

....Jacksonville, Florida

1. Pursuant to the requirements of sections 6036 and 6018 (a) of the Internal Revenue Code, notice is hereby given that: (*Executors or administrators fill in (a); custodians, joint owners, distributees, etc., fill in (b)*)

(*a*) The undersigned qualified as execut..or..../administrat............ of the estate of the above-named decedent in the
....County Judge's.................. Court at ......Clearwater, Florida.................. on
the ....20th.. .... day of ..December.............,1968.

(*b*) The undersigned, on or subsequent to the date of the decedent's death, had actual or constructive possession of property or of an interest in property which constituted a part of the decedent's gross estate, within the meaning of the estate tax law. The description and approximate value of such property at the time of death were as follows:

Description	Value
	$

2. To the best of the undersigned's knowledge the *approximate* values of the various classes of property (including any property not in possession of the undersigned) constituting the decedent's gross estate at date of death were as follows:

Real estate	$ 12,000.	Jointly owned property	$ 26,000.
Stocks and bonds	140,000.	Transfers during decedent's life	35,000.
Mortgages, notes, and cash	3,000.	General powers of appointment	0
Insurance on decedent's life	40,000.	All other property	500.
Annuities	0		
Total of above items		$ 256,500.	

3. The names and addresses of the legal representatives of the estate and their attorneys insofar as known to the undersigned are:

	Name	Address
Executors	Harry S. Smith	15 Sandy Road, Clearwater, Florida
Administrators		
Attorneys	Joseph Jones	201 Downtown Office Bldg.
		Clearwater, Florida

The undersigned HEREBY CERTIFIES that the instructions on the reverse side of this form have been carefully read and that all the statements made herein are correct to the best of the undersigned's knowledge and belief.

(Address) ..15 Sandy Road, Clearwater, Fla.(Signature) *Harry S. Smith*

Harry S. Smith

(Designation) Executor
(Executor/administrator/custodian/or other person—see instructions
on back, "Persons required to file notice")

NOTICE.—Failure to file a required return on Form 706 within 15 months from the date of death may render executors, administrators, and persons in actual or constructive possession of the decedent's property liable for penalties.

46

INSTRUCTIONS

Estates as to which notice is required.—This notice must be filed for the estate of every citizen or resident of the United States, whose gross estate (as defined by the statute) exceeded $60,000 in value at the date of death.

Form 705, instead of Form 704, must be filed for the estate of every nonresident not a citizen of the United States, if the part of his gross estate (as defined by the statute) situated in the United States exceeded a value of $2,000 at the date of death.

The value of the gross estate at the date of the decedent's death governs the liability for the filing of this notice, regardless of any valuation as of a subsequent time that may be adopted by the executor under the provisions of section 2032 of the Internal Revenue Code.

As the filing of the notice does not fix the tax liability, all doubt should be resolved in favor of giving notice.

Time for filing notice.—This notice must be filed within 2 months after the decedent's death, except that, if an executor or administrator qualifies within such period, the notice may be filed within 2 months after his qualification.

Persons required to file notice.—The duly qualified executor or administrator, or any person in actual or constructive possession of property included in the statutory gross estate, must file this notice, as follows: (1) The executor or administrator, qualified under an appointment by a court, must file the notice unless at the time of his qualification the notice has already been filed. (2) Any person in actual or constructive possession of property included in the statutory gross estate, must file the notice unless an executor or administrator qualifies within 2 months after the decedent's death. Persons in actual or constructive possession of such property include custodians, fiduciaries, transferees, joint owners, partners, distributees, debtors, agents, factors, brokers, bankers, safe deposit companies, and warehouse companies.

The signature of one executor or administrator upon this form is sufficient.

Execution of notice.—If this notice is filed by the executor or administrator, all information called for on face of this notice, except (*b*) of paragraph 1, should be furnished. If this notice is filed by a custodian, joint owner, distributee, etc., all information should be furnished, except (*a*) of paragraph 1.

If property includable in the gross estate (see paragraph 2 on face of this notice) consists of (1) property held jointly or in tenancy by the entirety, (2) property transferred during decedent's life, or (3) property subject to decedent's power of appointment, the approximate values thereof should be entered only under those headings, and not duplicated under the headings "Real estate," "Stocks and bonds," or "Mortgages, notes, and cash."

Place of filing.—In the case of a resident, this notice must be filed with the district director of internal revenue in whose district the decedent had his domicile at the time of death. In the case of a nonresident citizen, this notice must be filed with the Director of International Operations, Internal Revenue Service, Washington 25, D.C. In exceptional cases, application may be made to the Commissioner for permission to file in any other internal revenue district.

Gross estate.—The gross estate of decedents dying after October 16, 1962, as defined by section 2031(a) of the Internal Revenue Code, comprises property wherever situated including real property situated outside of the United States, unless the decedent's death was after October 16, 1962, and before July 1, 1964, and (i) the decedent's interest in the foreign real property was acquired before February 1, 1962, or (ii) the decedent's interest in the foreign real property was acquired after January 31, 1962, but the donor or prior decedent from whom the decedent's interest was acquired had acquired such prior interest before February 1, 1962. (The gross estate of decedents dying before October 17, 1962, does not include real property situated outside of the United States.) The gross estate includes—

1. Property in which the decedent at the time of his death had any beneficial interest.

2. Interest of surviving spouse, as dower, curtesy, or estate in lieu thereof.

3. Property transferred by the decedent during his life, by trust or otherwise (other than by bona fide sale for an adequate and full consideration in money or money's worth) as follows: (1) Transfers made in contemplation of death if made within 3 years prior to death; (2) transfers intended to take effect in possession or enjoyment at or after the decedent's death; (3) transfers under which the decedent reserved or retained (in whole or in part) the use, possession, rents, or other income, or enjoyment of the transferred property, for his life, or for a period not ascertainable without reference to his death, or for a period of such duration as to evidence an intention that it should extend to his death; including also the reservation or retention of the use, possession, rents, or other income, the actual enjoyment of which was to await the termination of a transferred precedent interest or estate; (4) transfers under which the decedent retained the right, either alone or in conjunction with another person or persons, to designate who should possess or enjoy the property or the income therefrom; and (5) transfers under which the enjoyment of the transferred property was subject at decedent's death to a change through the exercise, either by the decedent alone or in conjunction with another person or persons, of a power to alter, amend, revoke, or terminate, or where such a power was relinquished in contemplation of decedent's death.

4. Annuities received by any beneficiary by reason of surviving the decedent.

5. Property owned *jointly* or in *tenancy by the entirety*, with right of survivorship.

6. Property subject to a general power of appointment, including property with respect to which the decedent exercised or released the power during his lifetime.

7. Insurance upon the life of the decedent, including insurance receivable by beneficiaries other than the estate.

For more detailed information and exceptions as to property described in the preceding subparagraphs 3, 4, 5, 6, and 7, consult the Estate Tax Regulations under Chapter 11 of the Internal Revenue Code.

Lien.—Unless sooner paid in full, the tax is a lien for 10 years upon the entire gross estate, except such part thereof as is used for payment of charges against the estate and expenses of its administration allowed by any court having jurisdiction.

Penalties.—Criminal penalties for failure to file and for filing a false or fraudulent notice are provided by sections 7203, 7207, and 7269 of the Internal Revenue Code.

Delinquency.—In the event of failure to file notice within the time prescribed, a detailed explanation under oath or under penalty of perjury should accompany the notice when filed.

It is advisable to get an estimate of the fees and expenses in this situation. If at all possible, I would recommended a visit to view the property and a personal investigation as to its value.

36. SHOULD WIDOW FILE ELECTION:

Under the laws of the various states the widow, and sometimes the widower, is given the right to elect dower or a statutory share of the estate, if she is not satisfied with the provisions of the will. In other words, it is not possible to disinherit the widow against her wishes. The procedures and time limits depend upon state law.

Many modern wills are written making the widow the beneficiary of a trust. She may then face a difficult decision, for example, whether to take one-third outright, or take as the beneficiary of the trust.

The executor should point out the alternatives to the surviving spouse, so that she can make an intelligent decision. If she elects to take against the will, the distribution under the will is made as if she predeceased the testator.

37. CHECK FOR CLAIMS AND ESTABLISH RESERVES:

As indicated earlier, creditors of the deceased have a certain time within which to file claims against the estate. This is frequently six months, but you will have to check with your local authorities for exact time limits and procedures. If the claim is valid, you will pay it, if you have not already done so. If you feel it is not justified, you will, through your attorney, file an objection. You should check the court file for claims promptly upon the expiration of the creditors period, as there is a time limit on your filing your objection.

You may at this time want to establish a reserve fund for the payment of final court costs and expenses. If, however, the probate will be prolonged, you may want to postpone doing so until nearer the time for closing the estate. You establish this reserve by estimating your final costs, and showing in your accounting that you have paid this amount to yourself as a reserve for final costs. If there is any balance left after the final costs are paid, and you have received your discharge, you pay it over to the residuary beneficiaries.

38. PETITION FOR EXECUTOR'S AND ATTORNEY'S FEES:

As an executor you are entitled to a fee or commission for services rendered. Likewise your attorney is entitled to a fee for representing you in the probate of the estate. The method of computing these fees varies from state to state, according to local statute and custom. The executor's fees are usually based upon a percentage of the probate estate. A typical statute may allow 6% on the first $5,000; 4% on the next $5,000 and 2½% on all over $10,000.

There are two ways in which the court might approve the commissions and fees. By one method, the executor pays the commissions and reports them in his accounting to the Court. When the court approves the accounts he approves the fees. The second method, and the one which I favor, is to petition the court for allowance of fees, setting forth the facts in the petition, and obtaining a court order allowing the fees. The latter method is required in some jurisdictions.

In addition to the regular commissions, the law makes provision for payment for "extraordinary services." This may be described as services beyond those ordinarily required of an executor. There is a tremendous difference of opinion among professionals as to what constitutes extraordinary services. An example of such might be the operation of a business of which decedent was the sole proprietor. In any event, if you feel that the usual compensation is inadequate, you should discuss this with your attorney and the probate judge.

49

39. FILE ESTATE TAX RETURN:

For every estate which exceeds $60,000 in value at the time of death, a Federal Estate Tax return must be filed (Internal Revenue Service Form 706.) A sample form is reproduced herein, primarily to set out a suggested format. The instructions on the return itself are detailed and explicit, and if those instructions are followed, the return can be completed properly.

If the executor is reasonably skilled in following instructions, and competent with figures, he can do the return himself. If not, he may wish to have his accountant or attorney do it.

This return must be filed within fifteen months of the date of death. The executor has the privilege of using values as of the date of death, or one year after. The latter is called the alternate valuation date, and if used must be used throughout the return. If the alternate valuation date is used, any property sold during the year is returned at its sales price.

The various states tax estates or inheritances on various bases, so the executor should check with his local probate court to obtain the proper forms.

The executor has the privilege of asking the Internal Revenue Service for an early audit of the return and a release of personal liability. A letter of transmittal with a request for both follows:

> District Director of Internal Revenue
> City,
> State, ZIP
>
> > Re: Estate of John J. Smith
>
> Dear Sir:
>
> Enclosed herewith is IRS Form No. 706—Estate Tax Return, for the Estate of John J. Smith, and estate check in the amount of $11,618.93 in payment of the tax due.
>
> I desire to take advantage of Sections 2204 and

FORM **706** (Rev. Jan. 1966) U.S. TREASURY DEPARTMENT Internal Revenue Service	**UNITED STATES** **ESTATE TAX RETURN** Estates of nonresidents not citizens of the United States may generally file on Form 706NA instead of this form. For details see page 39.	**DO NOT WRITE IN SPACE BELOW** Date received

Decedent's first name and middle initial John J.	Decedent's last name Smith

Decedent's social security number 123-45-6789	Employer identification number for estate 56-123456

Date of death December 10, 1968	Citizenship (nationality) at time of death United States

Residence (domicile) at time of death
35 Beach Drive, Clearwater, Florida 33501

Did the decedent die testate? ☒ Yes ☐ No	Were letters testamentary or of administration granted for this estate? ☒ Yes ☐ No	Date granted Dec. 20, 1968

Case No. P-16421	Name of court County Judge's	Location of court Clearwater, Florida

To whom granted? (Designate whether executor, executrix, administrator, or administratrix. Explain if different from the person or persons filing return)

NAME	DESIGNATION	ADDRESS (Number, street, city, State, and Postal ZIP code)
Harry S. Smith	Executor	15 Sandy Road, Clearwater, Fla. 33502

COMPUTATION OF TAX
(See instructions on page 38)

Taxable estate (Item 5, Schedule P, or Item 9, Schedule Q, whichever is applicable) $68,378.43

PART I

1. Gross estate tax (use table A, page 40).. $11,845.96
2. Credit for State death taxes (use Table B, page 40) 227.03
3. Gross estate tax less credit for State death taxes (item 1 minus item 2). This is the net amount payable unless credit for Federal gift taxes, tax on prior transfers, or foreign death taxes is claimed in Part II............. $11,618.93

PART II

4. Credit for Federal gift taxes... $ 0
5. Credit for tax on prior transfers.. 0
6. Credit for foreign death taxes.. 0
7. Total of credits under Part II (total of items 4, 5, and 6)....................................
8. Net estate tax payable (item 3 minus item 7).. $11,618.93

(SPACE FOR USE OF INTERNAL REVENUE SERVICE)

Assessments					Payments		
Type of assessment (tax, interest, etc.)	Amount	List	Page	Line	Date	Principal	Interest
	$					$	$

DETERMINATION BY INTERNAL REVENUE SERVICE

Page 1

o59—16—77750-2

51

1. Address of decedent at time of death (Number, street, city, State, and Postal ZIP code)

35 Beach Drive, Clearwater, Florida 33501

2. State in which domiciled at time of death	**3.** Year in which this domicile was established
Florida	1959

4. Place of death	**5.** Cause of death	**6.** Length of last illness
Clearwater, Florida	Coronary Occlusion	3 days

7. Decedent's physicians

NAMES	ADDRESSES (Number, street, city, State, and Postal ZIP code)
James Hightower, M.D.	Medical Bldg., Clearwater, Fla., 33501

8. If decedent was confined in a hospital during his last illness or within 3 years prior to his death, give name and address of hospital

Clearwater Rest Home, Clearwater, Florida

9a. Date of birth	**9b.** Place of birth (City and State or country, if other than United States)
Feb. 9, 1898	Boston, Mass.

10a. Business or occupation	**10b.** If retired, state former business or occupation
retired	Engineer

10c. Business name	**10d.** Decedent's employer identification number, if any

10e. Business address (Number, street, city, State, and Postal ZIP code)
721 Old Church Place, Boston, Mass. 02101

11. Marital status of decedent at date of death

[X] Married [ ] Single [ ] Legally separated [ ] Widow or Widower [ ] Divorced

12a. Name of surviving husband or wife	**12b.** Social security number of surviving husband or wife
Mary Ann Smith	333-44-5555

12c. Date of marriage to surviving husband or wife	**12d.** Domicile at date of marriage to surviving husband or wife
June 10, 1920	Boston, Mass.

13a. If decedent was a widow or widower, give name of deceased husband or wife	**13b.** Date of death of deceased husband or wife

14. Individuals who receive benefits from the estate (do not include charitable beneficiaries shown in Schedule N or any heir receiving less than $1,000)

Name.—Enter the name of each individual who receives benefits from the estate directly as an heir, next-of-kin, devisee or legatee or indirectly (for example, as beneficiary of a trust, shareholder of a corporation or partner of a partnership which is an heir, etc.).

Social Security Number.—If the individual has no social security number, use his taxpayer account number.

Age.—On the date of the decedent's death.

Relationship.—Include relationships by blood, marriage, or adoption or indicate NONE.

Amount.—Value all interests on the date of death or the alternate valuation date, whichever is used for estate tax purposes. The interest of each beneficiary should be valued in the same manner as it would be valued for estate or gift tax purposes. Where precise values cannot readily be determined, a reasonable approximation should be entered. The sum of the values of the interests of all unborn or otherwise unascertainable beneficiaries should be shown on the last line (all unascertainable beneficiaries).

Name	Social Security Number	Age	Relationship to Decedent	Amount
Mary Ann Smith	333-44-5555	66	widow	138,378.43
John J. Smith, Jr.	123-65-6767	34	son	64,000.00
Shirley Smith	367-80-1006	28	daughter	64,000.00

All unascertainable beneficiaries 0

ESTATE OF . . . . John J. Smith . . . . Page 3

689—16—77750-2

52

15a. Did the decedent at date of death own property in any State or country other than that of his last domicile?   ☒ Yes   ☐ No
If "Yes," state place of ancillary probate proceedings

     Boston, Mass.

15b. Name of ancillary administrator or executor
     John J. Smith, Jr.

15c. Address of ancillary administrator or executor (Number, street, city, State, and Postal ZIP code)
     15 Exchange Place, Boston, Mass. 02101

16a. Did the decedent at the time of his death have a safe deposit box held either alone or in the joint names
of himself and another?   ☒ Yes   ☐ No
If "Yes," state location   First State Bank & Trust Co.,
                Clearwater, Florida

16b. If held jointly, give the name of the joint depositor
     Mary Ann Smith

16c. Relationship of joint depositor to decedent
     widow

16d. If the decedent had a safe deposit box at the time of his death, indicate by schedule and item number under what schedules in this
return the contents are listed
       B - 1 through 5
       C - 1 through 3
       F - 2 and 4

16e. If any of the contents of the safe deposit box are omitted from the schedules, explain fully why omitted
     Jewels belonging to decedent's widow.
     Miscellaneous papers having no value.

17. Did the undersigned person or persons filing return make diligent and careful search for property of every kind left
by the decedent?   ☒ Yes   ☐ No

18. Did the same undersigned make diligent and careful search for information as to any transfers (other than outright
transfers not in trust) of the value of $5,000 or more made by the decedent during his lifetime without an adequate
and full consideration in money or money's worth?   ☒ Yes   ☐ No

19. Did the same undersigned make diligent and careful search for the existence of any trusts created by the decedent
during his lifetime or any trusts created by other persons under which the decedent possessed any power, beneficial
interest, or trusteeship?   ☒ Yes   ☐ No

20a. Name of attorney representing estate, if any
     Joseph Jones

20b. Address (Number, street, city, State, and Postal ZIP code)   **20c.** Telephone No.
     201 Downtown Office Bldg.
     Clearwater, Fla., 33501   356-1235

ALTERNATE VALUATION

(These instructions apply only if alternate valuation is elected. For further information on this subject, see General Instructions
on page 4)

21. An election to have the gross estate of the decedent valued as of the alternate date or dates is made by entering a check mark in the
box set forth below.
☐ The executor elects to have the gross estate of this decedent valued in accordance with values as of a date or dates subsequent to the decedent's death as authorized by section 2032 of the Code.

ESTATE OF _____   Page 5

GROSS ESTATE
SCHEDULE A
REAL ESTATE

Did the decedent, at the time of his death, own any real estate required to be included in the gross estate? See General
Instruction J, page 4.   ☒ Yes   ☐ No

Item No.	Description	Subsequent valua-tion date	Alternate value	Value at date of death
1	House and Lot, 13 - 126th Ave., Boston Mass., Lot No. 56, (Old Addition) Single family residence - frame construction on 40' x 65' lot appraisal attached		$	$ 12,000
	Rental for Dec. 1968 due but not collected			55
	TOTAL (also enter under the Recapitulation, Schedule O)		$	$ 12,055

(If more space is needed, insert additional sheets of same size)

ESTATE OF ..... John J. Smith ....   Schedule A—Page 7

e59—11b 777.30-1

54

1. Did the decedent, if a resident or citizen of the United States, own any stocks or bonds, regardless of physical location, at the time of his death? ☒ Yes ☐ No

2. Did the decedent, if a nonresident not a citizen of the United States, own, at the time of his death, any stocks of corporations organized in the United States or bonds situated in the United States as explained in the instructions? ☐ Yes ☒ No

Item No.	Description (including face amount of bonds or number of shares)	Par	Unit value	Subsequent valuation date	Alternate value	Value at date of death
	STOCKS				$	$
1	200 shs American Tel & Tel Co. Com. NYSE	16 2/3	49½			9,900.00
2	1000 shs Bell & Howell Co. Com. NYSE	No	51			51,000.00
3	1000 shs Gen. Motors Corp. Com NYSE	1 2/3	66			66,000.00
	Dividend on item #2 of 1.50 payable Dec. 28 to holders of record Dec. 5					1,500.00
4	10 shs ABC Engineering Co. cap. Clearwater, Fla. Not listed Appraisal attached	No	2000			20,000.00
	BONDS					
5	$5,000 U.S. Treas. 4% due 1976 - Int. June & Dec. 30.	1000	91			4,550.00
	Interest accrued to Dec. 10, 1968					88.89
	TOTAL (also enter under the Recapitulation, Schedule O)				$	$153,038.89

(If more space is needed, insert additional sheets of same size)

ESTATE OF .... John J. Smith ....

Schedule B—Page 9

SCHEDULE C
MORTGAGES, NOTES, AND CASH

Did the decedent, at the time of his death, own any mortgages, notes, or cash? ☒ Yes ☐ No

Item No.	Description	Subsequent valuation date	Alternate value	Value at date of death
1	Note of Peter Wainwright dated Dec. 10, 1967 secured by mortgage on Lot 10, Excell Subd. Clearwater, Fla. Balance $2000 - 5% per annum due Dec. 10, 1970. Discount value		$	$
	Accrued interest to Dec. 10, 1968			1850.00 100.00
2	Balance in personal checking account at First State Bank & Trust Co., Clearwater, Florida			1250.00
3	Cash in possession of decedent			23.47
	TOTAL (also enter under the Recapitulation, Schedule O)		$	$3223.47

(If more space is needed, insert additional sheets of same size)

ESTATE OF ___John J. Smith_____

o60—16—77750-1

SCHEDULE D
INSURANCE

1a. Was any insurance on life of decedent receivable by his estate? ☒ Yes ☐ No

1b. By beneficiaries other than estate? ☒ Yes ☐ No

2. Was there any insurance on the decedent's life which is not included in the return as a part of the gross estate?
☒ Yes ☐ No   If "Yes," a complete explanation as to all such insurance must be submitted.

Item No.	Description	Subsequent valuation date	Alternate value	Value at date of death
1	$10,000 Everyman's Life Ins. Co., Albany, N.Y., policy No. 35701 payable to estate in one lump sum Form 712 attached		$	$ 10,000.00
2	$30,000 Mutual Ins. Co., Tallahassee, Florida, policy No. 78910 payable to estate in one lump sum. Form 712 attached			30,000.00
3	$25,000 Central Ins. Co., Orlando, Fla policy No. 36891 proceeds of $25,000 payable to decedent's widow, Mary Ann Smith who had all of the incidents of ownership. Form 712 attached			-- --- --
	TOTAL (also enter under the Recapitulation, Schedule O)		$	$ 40,000.00

(If more space is needed, insert additional sheets of same size)

ESTATE OF   John J. Smith

659—16—77750-1

SCHEDULE E

JOINTLY OWNED PROPERTY

I. Did the decedent, at the time of his death, own any property as a joint tenant or as a tenant by the entirety, with right of survivorship? ☒ Yes ☐ No
If "Yes," state the name and address of each surviving cotenant.

NAME	ADDRESS (Number, street, city, State, and Postal ZIP code)
Mary Ann Smith	35 Beach Drive
	Clearwater, Fla. 33501

Item No.	Description	Subsequent valuation date	Alternate value	Value at date of death
1	House and Lot at 35 Beach Drive, Clearwater, Fla., described as Lot No. Second Beach Subd. CBS Single family residence used as decedent's homeplace. Appraisal attached	10	$	$ 21,000.00
2	Contents of homeplace Appraisal attached			5,000.00
	TOTAL (also enter under the Recapitulation, Schedule O)		$	$26,000.00

(If more space is needed, insert additional sheets of same size)

ESTATE OF .....John J. Smith.. Schedule E—Page 15

a59—16—77750-1

SCHEDULE F
OTHER MISCELLANEOUS PROPERTY

1. Did the decedent, at the time of his death, own any interest in a copartnership or unincorporated business?
☐ Yes ☒ No

2. Did the decedent, at the time of his death, own any miscellaneous property not returnable under any other schedule?
☒ Yes ☐ No

3. Was there any insurance which the decedent owned on the life of another which is not included in the return as a part of the gross estate? If "Yes," full details must be submitted under this schedule. ☐ Yes ☒ No

4. State whether the decedent's estate, his spouse, or any other person, has received, or will receive, any bonus or award as a result of the decedent's employment or his death. If "Yes," full details must be submitted under this schedule. ☐ Yes ☒ No

Item No	Description	Subsequent valuation date	Alternate value	Value at date of death
1	Man's wrist watch		$	$ 55.00
2	2 carat diamond ring			1750.00
3	1966 Buick Sedan automobile			2700.00
4	Diamond Stick Pin			70.00
5	1922 Cord Convertible			2000.00

TOTAL (also enter under the Recapitulation, Schedule O) $ | $ 6575.00

(If more space is needed, insert additional sheets of same size)

ESTATE OF ....John J. Smith..

Schedule F—Page 17

o59—16—77730-1

59

SCHEDULE G
TRANSFERS DURING DECEDENT'S LIFE

1. Did the decedent make any transfer described in the first paragraph (including the six subparagraphs) of the instructions for this schedule?   ☒ Yes ☐ No

2a. Did the decedent, at any time, make a transfer (other than an outright transfer not in trust) of an amount of $5,000 or more without an adequate and full consideration in money or money's worth, but not believed to be includible in the gross estate as indicated in the first paragraph (including the six subparagraphs) of the instructions for this schedule?
If "Yes," furnish the following information: ☐ Yes ☒ No

2b. Date	**2c.** Amount or value	**2d.** Character of transfer

3a. Did the decedent, within 3 years immediately preceding his death, make any transfer of his property without an adequate and full consideration in money or money's worth?
If "Yes," and the transfer was of an amount of $1,000 or more, furnish the following information: ☒ Yes ☐ No

3b. Date	**3c.** Amount or value	**3d.** Character of transfer
See below		

3e. Motive which actuated decedent in making transfer
Love and affection

4. Were there in existence at the time of the decedent's death any trusts created by him during his lifetime?   ☐ Yes ☒ No

5. If a Federal gift tax return(s) was ever filed, state the year(s) covered and the Internal Revenue district in which filed.
1967 - Jacksonville, Florida

Item No.	Description	Subsequent valuation date	Alternate value	Value at date of death
1	On December 25, 1967 decedent made gifts of cash to his children:		$	$
	John J. Smith, Jr.			20,000.
	Shirley Smith			15,000.
	TOTAL (also enter under the Recapitulation, Schedule O)		$	$35,000.

(If more space is needed, insert additional sheets of same size)

ESTATE OF John J. Smith   Schedule G—Page 19

e59—16—77750-2

SCHEDULE H
POWERS OF APPOINTMENT

1a. Did the decedent at the time of death, possess a general power of appointment created after October 21, 1942? ☐ Yes ☒ No | **1b.** On or before such date? ☐ Yes ☒ No

2a. Did the decedent, at any time, by will or otherwise, exercise or release (to any extent) a general power of appointment created after October 21, 1942? ☐ Yes ☒ No | **2b.** On or before such date? ☐ Yes ☒ No

3. Were there in existence at the time of the decedent's death any trusts not created by him under which he possessed any power, beneficial interest, or trusteeship? ☐ Yes ☒ No

Item No.	Description	Subsequent valuation date	Alternate value	Value at date of death
1			$	$
	TOTAL (also enter under the Recapitulation, Schedule O)		$	$

(If more space is needed, insert additional sheets of same size)

SCHEDULE I
ANNUITIES

1a. Was the decedent, immediately before his death, receiving an annuity as described in paragraph 1 of the instructions? ☒ Yes ☐ No

1b. If "Yes," was that annuity paid pursuant to an approved plan as described in paragraph 4 of the instructions? ☐ Yes ☒ No

1c. If the answer to "1b." is "Yes," state the ratio of the decedent's contribution to the total purchase price of the annuity.

2a. If the decedent was employed at the time of his death, did an annuity or other payment as described in paragraph 3(d) of the instructions become payable to any beneficiary by reason of the beneficiary's having survived the decedent? ☐ Yes ☒ No

2b. If "Yes," state the ratio of the decedent's contribution to the total purchase price of the annuity.

Item No.	Description	Subsequent valuation date	Alternate value	Value at date of death
1	Gentleman's Life Insurance Co., Atlanta, Ga., Annuity Contract No. A-1756, dated 6-1-50; Annual installments of $900.00 to decedent for his life than to his widow for life.		$	$
	Value of annuity as obtained from Company			17,356.00
	TOTAL (also enter under the Recapitulation, Schedule O)		$	$ 17,356.00

(If more space is needed, insert additional sheets of same size)

ESTATE OF ...... John J. Smith ... . | Schedules H and I—Page 21

61

DEDUCTIONS

SCHEDULE J

FUNERAL EXPENSES AND EXPENSES INCURRED IN ADMINISTERING PROPERTY SUBJECT TO CLAIMS

NOTE.—Do not list on this schedule expenses of administering property not subject to claims. In connection with such expenses, see Schedule L.

If executors' commissions, attorneys' fees, etc., are claimed and allowed as a deduction for estate tax purposes, they are not allowable as a deduction in computing the taxable income of the estate for Federal income tax purposes.

Item No.	Description		Amount
	A. Funeral expenses:	$	
	O'Dell's Mortuary, Clearwater, Fla.	1,400.00	
	Ogle's Monument Co., Clearwater, Fla.	225.00	
	Total...	x x x x x x x x	$1,625.00
	B. Administration expenses.		
1	Executors' commissions—amount estimated XXXXXXXXXX. (Strike out words not applicable)...	x x x x x x x x	6,000.00
2	Attorneys' fees—amount estimated/XXXXXXXXXX (Strike out words not applicable)..	x x x x x x x x	6,800.00
3	Miscellaneous expenses:		
	Diamond Jewelry Co., Clearwater, Fla. appraisal		10.00
	Clay Calhoun, Realtor, Clearwater, Fla. "		75.00
	Tobias Hunter, " , Boston, Mass. "		25.00
	3 & X Appraisal Co., Jacksonville, Fla. appraisal of ABC Engineering Co. Stock		250.00
	County Judge's Court, court costs paid		78.00
	Estimated final costs and expenses		200.00
	Total miscellaneous expenses..................	x x x x x x x x	

TOTAL (also enter under the Recapitulation, Schedule O) | $ 15,063.00

(If more space is needed, insert additional sheets of same size)

ESTATE OF .... John J. Smith ....

o89—16—77750—2

SCHEDULE K

DEBTS OF DECEDENT AND MORTGAGES AND LIENS

Item No.	Debts of Decedent—Creditor and nature of claim, and allowable death taxes	Amount
1	Director of Internal Revenue - final income tax	$ 875.00
2	General Telephone Co. - final bill	17.35
3	James Hightower, M.D., Clearwater, Florida	378.00
4	Clearwater Rest Home, " "	130.00
5	Colbert Drug Co. " "	28.15
	TOTAL (also enter under the Recapitulation, Schedule O)	$1,428.50

Item No.	Mortgages and liens—Description	Amount
1	None	$
	TOTAL (also enter under the Recapitulation, Schedule O)	$ None

(If more space is needed, insert additional sheets of same size)

ESTATE OF ... John J. Smith

c59—16—77750-2

SCHEDULE L

NET LOSSES DURING ADMINISTRATION AND EXPENSES INCURRED IN ADMINISTERING PROPERTY NOT SUBJECT TO CLAIMS

Item No.	Net losses during administration	Amount
1	None	$
	TOTAL (also enter under the Recapitulation, Schedule O)	$None

Item No.	Expenses incurred in administering property not subject to claims (Indicate whether estimated, agreed upon, or paid.)	Amount
1	None	$
	TOTAL (also enter under the Recapitulation, Schedule O)	$None

(If more space is needed, insert additional sheets of same size)

ESTATE OF   John J. Smith   Schedule L—Page 27

o09—10—77760—1

64

SCHEDULE M

BEQUESTS, ETC., TO SURVIVING SPOUSE (MARITAL DEDUCTION)

If the decedent died testate, the person or persons filing the return should answer the following questions. Only question 4 should be answered in case the decedent died intestate. If the answer to any question is "Yes," full details should be submitted with the return.

1. Has any action been instituted to contest the will or any provision thereof affecting any property interest listed on this schedule or for construction of the will or any such provision? ☐ Yes ☒ No

2a. Had the surviving spouse the right to declare an election between (i) the provisions made in his or her favor by the will and (ii) dower, curtesy, or a statutory interest? ☒ Yes ☐ No

2b. If answer to question 2a is "Yes," has the surviving spouse renounced the will and elected to take dower, curtesy, or a statutory interest? ☐ Yes ☒ No | 2c. Elected to take under the will. ☒ Yes ☐ No

2d. Does the surviving spouse contemplate renouncing the will and electing to take dower, curtesy, or a statutory interest? ☐ Yes ☒ No

3. According to the information and belief of the person or persons filing the return, is any action described under question 1 designed or contemplated? ☐ Yes ☒ No

4. According to the information and belief of such person or persons, has any person other than the surviving spouse asserted (or is any such assertion contemplated) a right to any property interest listed on this schedule, other than as indicated under questions 1 or 3? ☐ Yes ☒ No

Item No.	Description of property interests passing to surviving spouse	Value
1	House and Lot at 35 Beach Drive, Clearwater, Florida (Item 1, Schedule E)	$ 21,000.00
2	Contents of homeplace (Item 2 Schedule E)	5,000.00
3	Tangible personal property bequeathed under Item III of decedent's will - (Items 1 through 5 of Schedule F)	6,575.00
4	Survivor's interest in Gentleman's Life Insurance Co. annuity (Item 1 of Schedule I)	17,356.00
5	Interest in "Marital Trust" created by Item IV of decedent's will	88,447.43

TOTAL.. $ 138,378.43

Less: (a) Federal estate tax payable out of above-listed property interests.............. $ None

(b) Other death taxes payable out of above-listed property interests.............. None

Total of items (a) and (b) 0.00

Net value of above-listed property interests (also enter under the Recapitulation, Schedule O)............... $ 138,378.43

(If more space is needed, insert additional sheets of same size)

ESTATE OF ....John J. Smith.. Schedule M—Page 29

e/9—16—77750-1

65

SCHEDULE N
CHARITABLE, PUBLIC, AND SIMILAR GIFTS AND BEQUESTS

If the transfer was made by will—

(a) Has any action been instituted to have interpreted or to contest the will or any provision thereof affecting the charitable deductions claimed in this schedule? ☐ Yes ☒ No

(b) According to the information and belief of the person or persons filing the return, is any such action designed or contemplated? ☐ Yes ☒ No

Item No.	Name and address of beneficiary	Character of institution	Amount
1	Most Holy Church, Clearwater, Florida	Religious	$ 10,000

TOTAL.. $ 10,000

Less: (a) Federal estate tax payable out of above-listed property interests .... $........0........

(b) Other death taxes payable out of above-listed property interests ....0........

Total of items (a) and (b).. 0

Net value of above-listed property interests (also enter under the Recapitulation, Schedule O)............... $ 10,000

(If more space is needed, insert additional sheets of same size)

ESTATE OF ..John J. Smith.. Schedule N—Page 31

●58—16—77730-2

SCHEDULE O
RECAPITULATION

Sched-ule	Gross estate	Alternate value	Value at date of death
A	Real estate..	$................	$ 12,055.00
B	Stocks and bonds...		153,038.89
C	Mortgages, notes, and cash....................................		3,223.47
D	Insurance..		40,000.00
E	Jointly owned property..		26,000.00
F	Other miscellaneous property..................................		6,575.00
G	Transfers during decedent's life..............................		35,000.00
H	Powers of appointment..		0.00
I	Annuities..		17,356.00
	TOTAL GROSS ESTATE....................................	$	$293,248.36

Sched-ule	Deductions	Amount	
J	1. Funeral expenses and expenses incurred in administering property subject to claims..	$ 15,063.00	
K	2. Debts of decedent...	1,428.50	
K	3. Mortgages and liens.......................................	.00	
	4. Total of items 1 through 3.................................	$ 16,491.50	
	5. Allowable amount of deductions from item 4 (see note*)..........	$ 16,491.50	
L	6. Net losses during administration............................	0.00	
L	7. Expenses incurred in administering property not subject to claims..............	0.00	
	8. Total of items 5 through 7.................................		$ 16,491.50
M	9. Bequests, etc., to surviving spouse..........................	$138,378.43	
	10. Adjusted gross estate (see note**).........................	276,756.86	
	11. Net amount deductible for bequests, etc., to surviving spouse (item 9 or one-half of item 10, whichever is smaller)...............................		138,378.43
N	12. Charitable, public, and similar gifts and bequests..............		10,000.00
	TOTAL ALLOWABLE DEDUCTIONS, except exemption (totals of lines 8 11, and 12).....................		$164,869.93

*Note.—See paragraph 1 of the instructions.
**Note.—Enter at item 10 the excess of "TOTAL GROSS ESTATE" over item 8, if the decedent and his surviving spouse at no time held property as community property. If property was ever held as community property, compute the "Adjusted gross estate" (item 10) in accordance with the instructions and example on page 32, and attach an additional sheet showing such computation.

ESTATE OF .....John J. Smith..................................   . . . .   Schedule O—Page 33

e59—16—77730—1

67

SCHEDULE P

TAXABLE ESTATE—RESIDENT OR CITIZEN

Instructions.—This Schedule Should be Used only for the Estate of a Resident or Citizen of the United States

1. Total gross estate...		$293,248.36
2. Total allowable deductions...	$164,869.93	
3. Exemption...	60,000.00	
4. Total deductions plus exemption...		224,869.93
5. Taxable estate (item 1 minus item 4)...		$ 68,378.43

SCHEDULE Q

TAXABLE ESTATE—NONRESIDENT NOT A CITIZEN OF THE UNITED STATES

Instructions.—This schedule should be used only for the estate of a nonresident not a citizen of the United States. See instructions under "Deduction of administration expenses, claims, etc.," on page 39. See also instructions under **"Exemption"** on page 39 for amount of exemption and names of countries, the estates of whose residents qualify for the **"prorated exemption."** If decedent was domiciled in Canada and died after December 31, 1958, see **"Convention with Canada"** on page 39 regarding special exemption and tax computation. Use Form 706g (Schedule Q (2)) instead of Schedule Q in case of decedent who at the time of his death was domiciled in France or Greece and was not a citizen of the United States. (If the "prorated exemption" is claimed under the Japanese convention, the numerator of the fraction set forth in item 7 is the value of the property situated in the United States and subjected to tax by both Japan and the United States.) The value to be entered for item 2 includes real property situated outside of the United States if required to be included in the gross estate by General Instruction J, page 4.

1. Value of gross estate in the United States (Schedules A, B, C, D, E, F, G, H, and I)............................	$................
2. Value of gross estate outside the United States (must be supported by proof described in instructions under "Deduction of administration expenses, claims, etc.," on page 39)............................	_____
3. Value of total gross estate wherever situated (item 1 plus item 2)............................	$_____
4. Gross deductions under Schedules J, K, and L............................	$_____
5. Net deductions under Schedules J, K, and L (that proportion of item 4 that item 1 bears to item 3).............	$................
6. Charitable, public, and similar gifts and bequests (Schedule N)............................	_____
7. Exemption of $2,000 (in estates qualifying for "prorated exemption," use $2,000 or $\frac{\text{item 1}}{\text{item 3}} \times \$60,000$, whichever is the greater)............................	_____
8. Total deductions plus exemption (item 5 plus items 6 and 7)............................	$_____
9. Taxable estate (item 1 minus item 8)............................	$

SCHEDULE R

CREDIT FOR TAX ON PRIOR TRANSFERS

Name of transferor	Date of transferor's death

Transferor's residence at time of death

COMPUTATION OF THE CREDIT

PART I—TRANSFEROR'S TAX ON PRIOR TRANSFERS

1. Net value of transfers............................	$_____
2. Value of transferor's estate (adjusted in accordance with instructions for item 2)............................	$_____
3. Tax on transferor's estate (adjusted in accordance with instructions for item 3)............................	$_____
4. Transferor's tax on prior transfers (proportion of item 3 which item 1 bears to item 2)............................	$_____

PART II—TRANSFEREE'S TAX ON PRIOR TRANSFERS

5. Transferee's tax computed without regard to credit allowed under this schedule............................	$_____
6. Transferee's reduced gross estate............................	$_____
7. Transferee's deductions (adjusted in accordance with instructions for item 7)............................	_____
8. Transferee's reduced taxable estate (item 6 minus item 7)............................	$................
9. Tax on reduced taxable estate............................	$_____
10. Transferee's tax on prior transfers (item 5 minus item 9)............................	$_____

PART III—CREDIT ALLOWABLE

11. Maximum amount before application of percentage requirement (item 4 or item 10, whichever is smaller).........	$_____
12. Percent allowable is	
13. Credit allowable (item 12 × item 11)............................	$

ESTATE OF .... John J. Smith ....

Schedule P, Q, and R—Page 35

o59—16—77730-1

(b) Computation of credit in cases where property is situated outside both countries or deemed situated within both countries.— In such cases consult the appropriate treaty for details.

5. Example of computation of credit under the Statute.—The decedent was a citizen of, and domiciled in, the United States at the time of his death. The gross estate consisted of real property in M country valued at $60,000; stocks of United States corporations, $90,000; bonds of corporations organized under the laws of M country, $45,000; and stocks of corporations organized under the laws of M country, $75,000. On the date of death, all of the stock and bond certificates were in a bank vault in the United States. Debts and administration expenses total $20,000. The M country real property valued at $60,000 and $10,000 of the stocks of M country corporations passed to the decedent's surviving spouse and the latter items qualified for and were allowed as a marital deduction. The amount of the gross Federal estate tax less credit for State inheritance taxes is $25,820. The amount of the M country inheritance tax imposed on the widow's inheritance of $70,000 is $21,000. The value of the daughter's inheritance is $65,000, consisting entirely of stocks of M country corporations. The amount of the M country inheritance tax imposed on the daughter's inheritance is $19,500. M country did not impose inheritance tax on the bonds issued by the M country corporations.

Schedule S is filled out as follows:

1. Amount of estate, inheritance, legacy and succession taxes imposed in the above country attributable to property situated in that country, and subjected to such taxes, and included in the gross estate (as defined by statute)	$40,500.00
2. Value of the gross estate (adjusted)	$200,000.00
3. Value of property situated in that country, and subjected to death taxes imposed in that country, and included in the gross estate (adjusted)	$65,000.00
4. Federal estate tax before allowance of credit for foreign death taxes	$25,820.00
5. Amount of Federal estate tax attributable to property specified at item 4 that item 3 bears to item 2)	$8,391.50
6. Credit for death taxes imposed in the above country (item 1 or item 5, whichever is the smaller)	$8,391.50

SCHEDULE S

CREDIT FOR FOREIGN DEATH TAXES

List all of the foreign countries to which death taxes have been paid, credit for the payment of which is claimed on this return .. ..

If credit is claimed for death taxes paid to more than one foreign country, compute the credit for taxes paid to one country on this sheet and use a separate copy of Schedule S for each of the other countries. The copies of Schedule S on which the additional computations are made should be attached hereto.

The credit computed on this sheet is for ....
(Name of death tax or taxes)

.... imposed in ....
(Name of country)

Credit is computed under the ....
(Insert "treaty" or "statute")

COMPUTATION OF THE CREDIT

(All amounts and values shown hereunder must be entered in United States money)

1. Amount of estate, inheritance, legacy and succession taxes imposed in the above country attributable to property situated in that country, and subjected to such taxes, and included in the gross estate (as defined by statute) .... $..........................

2. Value of the gross estate (adjusted, if necessary, in accordance with Instructions for item 2) .... $..........................

3. Value of property situated in that country, and subjected to death taxes imposed in that country, and included in the gross estate (adjusted, if necessary, in accordance with instructions for item 3) .... $..........................

4. Federal estate tax before allowance of credit for foreign death taxes .... $..........................

5. Amount of Federal estate tax attributable to property specified at item 3 (proportion of item 4 that item 3 bears to item 2) .... $..........................

6. Credit for death taxes imposed in the above country (item 1 or item 5, whichever is the smaller) .... $..........................

ESTATE OF .. .. John J. Smith .... Schedule S—Page 37

e5₉—16—777.30-2

DECLARATION

Under penalty of perjury, I declare that this return, including any accompanying statements, has been examined by me, and **is**, to the best of my knowledge and belief, a true, correct, and complete return, made in good faith pursuant to the Internal Revenue Code and the regulations thereunder.

Jan. 15, 1970   *Harry S. Smith*   15 Sandy Road,
(Date)   (Signature of executor, administrator, etc.)   (Address)

            HARRY S. SMITH   Clearwater, Fla. 33502

DECLARATION OF ATTORNEY OR AGENT PREPARING RETURN

Under penalties of perjury, I declare that I prepared this return for the person or persons whose signature(s) appear(s) above and that this return, including any accompanying schedules and statements, is, to the best of my knowledge and belief, a true, correct and complete return based on all the information relating to the matters required to be reported in this return of which I have any knowledge.

(Date)   (Signature of preparer (individual or firm) other than   (Address)
executor, administrator, etc.)

TABLE A

COMPUTATION OF GROSS ESTATE TAX

Taxable estate equal to or more than—	Taxable estate less than—	Tax on amount in column (1)	Rate of tax on excess over amount in column (1)
(1)	(2)	(3)	(4)
			(Percent)
0	$5,000	0	3
$5,000	10,000	$150	7
10,000	20,000	500	11
20,000	30,000	1,600	14
30,000	40,000	3,000	18
40,000	50,000	4,800	22
50,000	60,000	7,000	25
60,000	100,000	9,500	28
100,000	250,000	20,700	30
250,000	500,000	65,700	32
500,000	750,000	145,700	35
750,000	1,000,000	233,200	37
1,000,000	1,250,000	325,700	39
1,250,000	1,500,000	423,200	42
1,500,000	2,000,000	528,200	45
2,000,000	2,500,000	753,200	49
2,500,000	3,000,000	998,200	53
3,000,000	3,500,000	1,263,200	56
3,500,000	4,000,000	1,543,200	59
4,000,000	5,000,000	1,838,200	63
5,000,000	6,000,000	2,468,200	67
6,000,000	7,000,000	3,138,200	70
7,000,000	8,000,000	3,838,200	73
8,000,000	10,000,000	4,568,200	76
10,000,000	....	6,088,200	77

TABLE B

COMPUTATION OF MAXIMUM CREDIT FOR STATE DEATH TAXES

Taxable estate equal to or more than—	Taxable estate less than—	Credit on amount in column (1)	Rate of credit on excess over amount in column (1)
(1)	(2)	(3)	(4)
			(Percent)
0	$40,000	0	None
$40,000	90,000	0	0.8
90,000	140,000	$400	1.6
140,000	240,000	1,200	2.4
240,000	440,000	3,600	3.2
440,000	640,000	10,000	4.0
640,000	840,000	18,000	4.8
840,000	1,040,000	27,600	5.6
1,040,000	1,540,000	38,800	6.4
1,540,000	2,040,000	70,800	7.2
2,040,000	2,540,000	106,800	8.0
2,540,000	3,040,000	146,800	8.8
3,040,000	3,540,000	190,800	9.6
3,540,000	4,040,000	238,800	10.4
4,040,000	5,040,000	290,800	11.2
5,040,000	6,040,000	402,800	12.0
6,040,000	7,040,000	522,800	12.8
7,040,000	8,040,000	650,800	13.6
8,040,000	9,040,000	786,800	14.4
9,040,000	10,040,000	930,800	15.2
10,040,000	....	1,082,800	16.0

ESTATE OF .... John J. Smith

U.S. GOVERNMENT PRINTING OFFICE   o59—16—77750-1

6501(d) of the Internal Revenue Code. Pursuant thereto, I hereby make application for prompt assessment of the estate tax liability and discharge from personal liability as executor.

Please indicate your receipt hereof on the enclosed copy and return the copy in the envelope provided.

Very truly yours,

_____

Executor of the Estate of
John J. Smith

40. CONSIDER PAYMENT OF SPECIFIC LEGACIES AND PARTIAL DISTRIBUTION OF RESIDUE:

The executor cannot be compelled to distribute any property or pay any bequests until the creditors period expires, and it is dangerous to do so. In an estate not subject to estate tax, he should do so as soon thereafter as legally possible.

If the estate is subject to estate tax, the executor is within his rights to withhold distribution until the tax return is approved and he receives his release from personal liability. However, this may take up to twenty-seven months, so if he is confident that he can pay the specific bequests, and make a partial distribution of the residue, he may want to do so.

Since he makes this distribution at his own peril, he should withhold enough to take care of any contingencies, such as the internal revenue increasing the valuation in the tax return.

41. CONSIDER APPOINTMENT OF GUARDIAN OR GUARDIAN AD LITEM:

If there are beneficiaries of the estate who are minors or under legal disability, it will be necessary that they have a guardian.

A guardian is a person or institution appointed by the

court to look after the interests of the minor. Guardians are of three tpyes:

(1) Guardian of the Property (or estate)
(2) Guardian of the Person
(3) Guardian ad litem

The same person may be guardian of the property and of the person. Before the executor makes distribution to a person who is a minor or otherwise under legal disability, he should have a certified copy of the guardian's appointment in his file. He should advise the parents or other persons having custody of the minor to have a guardian appointed.

If there are minors or unknown beneficiaries who will not be receiving an immediate distribution, but who have an ultimate interest in the estate, the court should be petitioned to appoint a guardian ad litem. This means during the pendency of the suit. This occurs, for example, where a trust is to be established under the will, with the remainder after a life estate to be paid to lineal descendants. The guardian ad litem is appointed to protect the interests of the ultimate and perhaps unknown beneficiaries.

A guardian ad litem will also be necessary where the interests of the testamentary or natural guardian are adverse to the infant's. An example of this is where the widow is executor of the husband's estate and also guardian of the minor children.

It is possible in some states to have the disabilities of non-age removed by court action if the minor is over a certain age, for example, eighteen years. This may be desirable where the party is capable of handling his own property or the expense of a guardianship is sought to be avoided.

42. FILE ACCOUNTS WITH VOUCHERS:

The executor must prepare and file an accounting of his administration with the court when he is ready to petition the court for an order of distribution. All expenditures and distributions should be supported by signed vouchers, receipts or cancelled checks. Accompanying the accounting should be a schedule of assets on hand.

The accounting should be prepared in such a way that the court's auditor or clerk will be able to start with the inventory of the estate, follow the transactions through the accounting and arrive at the schedule of assets on hand. A simple form of accounting follows. The schedule of assets will be in substantially the same form as the inventory.

ESTATE OF JOSIAH BREADFRUIT

First and Final Account

Date	Explanation	Received	Disbursed
1967		$	$
8-15	Cash on decedent's person	102.12	
	Balance of checking account - First Nat'l Bank	1,204.68	
	Cash in safe deposit box #234 at " " "	300.00	
8-23	Rec'd div. on 100 shs A.T.& T. com.	150.00	
	Rec'd interest on $10M U.S. Treas. Bds		
	4% due 6/87	200.00	
8-29	Pd. Sun Valley Funeral Home		1,427.13
	Pd. Probate Judge - Court Costs		75.50
	Pd. Alvin Green, M.D.		750.00
	Pd. Elsie Smith, R.N.		112.00
1968			
2-15	Sold the following stocks:		
	100 shs A.T.& T. com. @ 51	5,100.00	
	100 shs Xerox Corp. com. @ 237	23,700.00	
2-16	Pd note at First National Bank -		
	Princ 10,000 plus interest 400		10,400.00
10-12	Pd. Federal Estate Tax		11,750.00
	Pd. Florida Estate Tax		1,111.00
10-14	Pd. Alex Good, Attorney's Fee		2,200.00
	Pd. John J. Jones, Executor's Fee		2,000.00
	Reserved for final court costs		100.00
10-15	Balance of cash on hand		831.17
	Totals	$30,756.80	$30,756.80

43. PETITION FOR ORDER OF DISTRIBUTION:

In the case of an intestate, i.e. without a will, this section could be entitled "Petition to Determine Heirs." It will be your duty as administrator to search for the heirs at law, and present proof to the court to support your findings.

It may also be necessary to determine heirship if one of the beneficiaries of the will has predeceased the testator, and the will does not provide for this contingency. If the deceased beneficiary was not related within a certain degree of kinship, the legacy is said to "lapse." This means that the legacy fails, and the bequest falls into the residue. If he does, however, fall within the degree of kinship set forth in the statute, his lineal descendants may inherit his share. The executor will have to make this determination, and present proofs to the court.

There are two ways in which an estate can be distributed, assuming the foregoing problems have been solved. Those two ways are: "In Cash" and "In Kind." To distribute cash is obviously very simple. To distribute "in kind" means to distribute the property as such, and this becomes a bit more complicated where there are multiple beneficiaries.

The executor must, in the latter situation, prepare a "Schedule of Distribution." This schedule sets forth the assets to be distributed to each beneficiary at their market value as of the date of distribution. Any minor differences are adjusted with cash. The date chosen for distribution must, of necessity, be arbitrary. Where there is a surviving widow taking "marital deduction" property, and interests in other assets going to others, the Internal Revenue regulations require that the assets so distributed fairly reflect any appreciation or depreciation occurring up to the date of distribution. For illustration in the following schedule I am assuming a widow taking 50 per cent of the estate and two children taking 25 per cent each. This schedule can be adapted to any similar situation. (see page 75)

44. DISTRIBUTE AND OBTAIN RECEIPTS:

Once the court order is obtained, the executor can distribute the remaining assets of the estate, and obtain receipts from the beneficiaries. The receipts should be in duplicate; one to be filed with the court, and one to be retained by the executor. A form of receipt is set out below.

If delivery can be made in person, the receipt can be obtained at the same time. However, a problem is presented

ESTATE OF JOE DOKE   SCHEDULE OF DISTRIBUTION   MARKET VALUE 7-12-69

Mrs. Mary Doke	50%	Joe Doke, Jr.	25%	Annie Doke	25%	100%
$5,000 U.S. Treasury Bonds due 7-1-87	$4,450.00	$5,000 U.S. Treasury Bonds due 7-1-87	$4,450.00		$	$8,900.00
Accrued int. on above	80.00	Accrued int. on above	80.00	Accrued int. on above	160.00	160.00
$5,000 U.S. Treasury Bonds due 8-15-85	4,475.00			$5,000 U.S. Treasury Bonds due 8-15-85	$4,475.00	8,950.00
Accrued int. on above	95.00			Accrued int. on above	95.00	190.00
100 Shs. Am. Tel. & Tel. Com.	5,100.00	50 Shs. Am. Tel. & Tel. Com.	2,550.00	50 Shs. Am. Tel. & Tel. Com.	2,550.00	10,200,00
50 Shs. Beth. Steel Com.	1,500.00	24 Shs. Beth. Steel Com.	720.00	28 Shs. Beth. Steel Com.	690.00	2,910.00
100 Shs. Motorola Com.	14,425.00	50 Shs. Motorola Com.	7,212.50	51 Shs. Motorola Com.	7,356.75	28,994.25
1/2 Undivided Interest in Doke Ranch	80,000.00	1/4 Undivided Interest in Doke Ranch	40,000.00	1/4 Undivided Interest in Doke Ranch	40,000.00	160,000.00
Cash	12,375.00	Cash	6,237.50	Cash	6,083.25	24,695.75
TOTALS	$122,500.00		$61,250.00		$61,250.00	$245,000.00

if the beneficiary lives out of town, and the assets must be shipped to him. The following letter suggests the method to be used:

Mrs. Elvira Goodway
Florala, Alabama

Re: Estate of Cornelius Goodway

Dear Mrs. Goodway:

I am now in a position of make distribution of the assets of the estate of Cornelius Goodway. Enclosed you will find a receipt setting forth the items which you will receive. Will you please sign and return to me two copies of the receipt, as I need one for the probate court and one for my file.

If you would rather not sign the receipt until you have the assets in hand, please give me the name of your local bank, and I will mail the securities to them, to be delivered to you upon their receiving the signed receipt.

Very truly yours,

If the bequest is one of cash, simply send the receipts with the check, as the check will serve as a receipt. The check should, however, contain an adequate description, such as: "In full payment of bequest under Item III of the will."

You may want to make exceptions to the rigidity of the foregoing method. If the beneficiary is represented by counsel, you might send the assets to him and rely on him to obtain the receipts; likewise, if the beneficiary is a charitable or public institution. This is, of course, a matter of common sense. In any event, make sure you have your receipts.

FORM OF RECEIPT

Estate of Cornelius Goodway, dec'd.

Receipt of Beneficiary

The undersigned acknowledges receipt from Harry

Young, Executor of the Estate of Cornelius Goodway, deceased, of the following items:

> 100 shs United States Steel Corp. com.
> stock—ctf. No. NY60578 reg. n/o
> Elvira Goodway.
> 1 Bar Pin containing 8 small diamonds.
> Signed and sealed the.............. .....day of
> ....(Seal)
> Elvira Goodway

Witnessed by:

....

....,...

If the items are difficut to identify, it is well to use both the language of the will, and the description used in the inventory. An example might be:

> Described in Item IV of the will as "Aunt Minnie's diamond ring," and also described as one "lady's dinner ring with one diamond of approximately 2 carats and six diamonds of approximately ⅛ carat each."

This will enable the court's auditors to trace the item from the will to the inventory to the receipt.

45. PAY FINAL COSTS, OBTAIN DISCHARGE AND DISTRIBUTE BALANCE:

After you have obtained the receipts of the beneficiaries, you will have your attorney file these receipts with the court. At this time, he will prepare a report of distribution and petition for final discharge.

After you have obtained a certified copy of.the order of final discharge, and paid the final court costs, you can distribute the balance in your reserve account to the residuary beneficiaries.

You may now relax in the satisfaction of a job well done.

PART 2

Wills And
Estate Planning

Having just been through the archaic procedures necessary to probate an estate, you can readily see the advisability of easing this burden. The term "estate planning" embraces the preparation of wills, and might be said to have two primary objectives—to provide for the orderly disposition of property according to the wishes of the testator; and to arrange for the descent of property with the lowest possible tax and at the least possible expense.

Although it is hazardous to be dogmatic on any subject, it is reasonably safe to say that every person of property should have a will. The first and most important function of a will is to enable a person to dispose of his property as he wishes. In the absence of a will, property descends by operation of law. These laws, which are called "Statutes of Descent and Distribution," are more or less compromises agreed upon in the various state legislatures. A typical statute might leave the widow one-third of her husband's property and divide the rest among his children. If the estate is a small one, the widow is not getting enough; if it is a large one, certain tax benefits are being lost.

A will can be drawn to take advantage of provisions of the federal estate tax laws, and where the estate is a large one this can mean a substantial saving for the family. For example, if a man leaves an estate of $200,000 to his wife outright, either by will or joint ownership, the combined taxes on his and his wife's estate could be as much as $36,060; whereas by the proper use of trusts, which can be for the benefit of his wife during her lifetime, the combined taxes could be reduced to $9,600. This amounts to a saving of $26,460 for the children.

As mentioned above, a will can incorporate a trust. This may be especially important where there are minor children or beneficiaries who are not competent to manage investments. A guardian may be designated in the will, but a trust has many advantages over a guardianship. A guardianship is generally a much more expensive method; guardian's powers of investment are more limited; and his freedom to act on behalf of the ward more restricted. A trustee can be given broad discretionary powers, which will enable him to act with little or no court supervision.

Wills are too often thought of only in connection with the elderly. The preceding paragraph points up the importance of a will for the young man who has minor children. When a young man adds up his estate, including his insurance, he is frequently surprised to find out how much he is worth. The will reproduced at the end of this section is an example of a will for such a person.

The example assumes an estate with no great tax problem; that the man is married and has a minor child. He wants to leave all of his estate to his wife, but wants to protect the children in the event of a common disaster. The wife should have a will with substantially the same provisions, in the event that she survives the husband, but cannot or does not make a later will. His insurance will be payable to his wife, with his estate as the secondary beneficiary. A will where there are no minors might be simpler;

a will for a taxable estate will be more complicated.

No one should copy a will from a book. Each person's situation is unique, and professional advice should be sought, not only in the actual preparation of the will, but in the planning stages. In order for your attorney to do an adequate job, you should go to him prepared. He should know the extent of your property, with approximate valuations. He should know how the titles are held, that is, whether in your name alone or as "joint tenants with right of survivorship." Only by having complete information can he do the job you hire him to do.

The red tape of probate can be reduced by properly drafted clauses in the will which either give the executor certain powers or relieve him of certain obligations otherwise required by law. The executor's job can be simplified, and the probate process streamlined by the will. Although the thought of a simple will may be appealing, from an administrative standpoint it can be troublesome. You will note that the accompanying example relieves the executor from posting bond, and gives her complete powers of sale and management. These are just two examples of what this paragraph is about.

There is another device which is well worth considering when planning an estate. This is known as the "Revocable Living Trust." The revocable living trust can be utilized to bypass the probate process. The same provisions can be incorporated in the trust as can be put in the will. In short, the trust agreement can act as a substitute for the will, and avoid the probate process and the consequent expense involved. The trust can be used in coordination with a "pour-over" will, which leaves all of the property not otherwise disposed of to the trust, to be managed and distributed accordingly.

A useful variation of the revocable living trust is known as a "Life Insurance Trust." This is highly desirable for a man with large amounts of life insurance. The trustee is named beneficiary of the policies, and collects the proceeds upon the death of the insured. The trustee thenceforth operates under the terms of the trust agreement. During the insured's lifetime, the trust is passive. The insured retains the right to withdraw the policies, cash them, or borrow on them. Actually, nothing happens until he dies.

There are numerous other estate planning devices which can be utilized to ease the burden of probate and save the family considerable sums of money. The professionals are constantly working on variations of wills and trusts to accomplish this end. There are two sources of advice which everyone should take advantage of: the attorney, and the bank trust officer. These two men, working in cooperation with the accountant and insurance agent, can design a program best suited to each individual's situation.

Men will exert their efforts for a lifetime accumulating an estate, and deny a few minutes to provide for its disposition. Hopefully, this tendency will be overcome in the future.

LAST WILL AND TESTAMENT
OF
JONATHAN FAST

I, JONATHAN FAST, a resident of Largo, County of Pinellas, and State of Florida, do hereby make, publish and declare this to be my Last Will and Testament.

ITEM ONE

I hereby revoke all wills and codicils made by me at any time heretofore.

ITEM TWO

I direct that all my just debts and funeral expenses be paid as soon as practicable after my death.

ITEM THREE

I direct that all estate, inheritance, transfer, legacy or succession taxes or death duties which may be assessed or imposed with respect to my estate or any part thereof wheresoever situate, whether or not passing under my will, shall be paid out of my residuary estate as an expense of administration and without apportionment.

ITEM FOUR

I give, devise and bequeath all the rest, residue and remainder of my property, both real and personal, whatsoever and wheresoever situate, to my wife MARY ANN FAST, to be hers absolutely and forever.

ITEM FIVE

If my wife predeceases me, I give all the rest, residue and remainder of my property, including the proceeds of all insurance policies on my life, to GEORGE JONES of Largo, Florida, and the XYZ NATIONAL BANK OF LARGO, as Trustees, IN TRUST, NEVERTHELESS, for the following uses and purposes:

(1) To hold, possess, invest and reinvest, manage and control said property in a trust to be known as the JONATHAN FAST trust.

(2) To pay so much of the income and principal of said trust to or for the benefit of my son, JONATHAN FAST, JR., for his support, education and welfare as, in their sole discretion, my Trustees deem advisable.

(3) Upon my son's attaining the age of twenty-five (25) years, one-half of the remaining trust estate shall be distributed to him. The other one-half shall be held according to the terms hereof until he attains the age of thirty (30) years and, at such time, that part shall be paid over to him free of this trust. If said trust estate should be less than $10,000 the Trustees may, in their discretion, distribute said trust estate to my son free of this trust provided he has attained the age of twenty-one (21) years. If my son should die before receiving final distribution hereof, I direct that the assets remaining in said trust be distributed to his lineal descendants, per stirpes.

(4) In the event that my son dies without lineal des-

cendants, then upon the death of the survivor of my wife and my son, the net income from the Trust Estate shall be divided equally between my mother, ELLEN FAST, and my mother-in-law, HELEN ALLEN, and distributed to them at quarterly or more frequent intervals. Upon the death of either, the entire net income shall be paid to the survivor. The Trustees may, at their sole discretion, distribute principal to or for the benefit of my mother and mother-in-law for their support and general welfare. Upon the death of both my mother and mother-in-law, the principal and any accumulated income shall be distributed to my living nieces and nephews and my wife's living nieces and nephews equally, share and share alike.

ITEM SIX
No income or principal payable to or held for any beneficiary under the terms hereof shall be alienated, disposed of or in any manner encumbered by such beneficiary while in the possession of the executor or trustees and any attempt to do so shall be null and void.

ITEM SEVEN
I hereby nominate, constitute and appoint my wife, MARY ANN FAST, and XYZ NATIONAL BANK OF LARGO, a corporation organized and existing under the laws of the United States, to be executors of this my LAST WILL AND TESTAMENT, both to serve without bond. In the event of my wife's death or incapacity, XYZ NATIONAL BANK OF LARGO, shall be the sole executor.

ITEM EIGHT
In addition to all other powers conferred by law and elsewhere herein granted, my executors and trustees shall have full power to receive, hold, manage, convert, sell, assign, alter, reinvest and otherwise deal with the properties in my estate and the trust herein created as they shall deem to be for the best interests of the beneficiaries hereunder

to the same extent that I myself might do if living, all without obtaining authority or confirmation from any court.

By way of illustration, but not of limitation of their powers, I hereby authorize my executors and trustees:

(1) To retain the original properties received by them for such time as they shall deem best, and to dispose of them by sale or exchange, or otherwise, as and when they shall deem advisable;

(2) To participate in the liquidation, reorganization, consolidation or other financial readjustment of any corporation or business in which my estate or the trust estate are or shall be financially interested;

(3) To determine what expenses and other charges shall be charged against principal and what against income;

(4) To invest any funds in such properties as they shall deem advisable even though they are not technically recognized as legal investments for fiduciaries:

(5) To borrow money for the benefit of my estate or the trust estate, and, if required to do so, secure the same by mortgage or collateral;

(6) To compromise, arbitrate or otherwise adjust claims in favor of or against my estate or the trust estate;

(7) To execute deeds, contracts, bills of sale, notes and other instruments in writing required for the businesslike administration of my estate or the trust estate;

(8) To receive all rents, profits, and income of every nature due my estate or the trust estate;

(9) To hold assets or investments in the name of a nominee;

(10) To make any division or distribution required under the terms of this will in money or in kind, or partly in money and partly in kind, without allocating the same kind of property to different shares or distributees, and the division made by my said executors or trustees and the values established by them for such division shall be binding and conclusive on all persons.

ITEM NINE

In the event of both my wife's and my death, and it is necessary that a guardian be appointed for my son, I direct that my brother, SAM FAST, be so appointed.

ITEM TEN

In the event that my wife and I die as a result of a common disaster, or under circumstances such that it cannot be readily determined who predeceased the other, it shall be presumed that my wife predeceased me.

ITEM ELEVEN

Anyone dealing with the executors or trustees is not required to see to the application the executors or trustees make of the funds or other properties they may receive.

IN WITNESS WHEREOF, I have hereunto set my hand and seal at Largo, Florida, this 15th day of August, 1968.

/s/ Jonathan Fast
JONATHAN FAST

The foregoing instrument was signed, sealed, published and declared by the above named testator as and for his LAST WILL AND TESTAMENT, in the presence of us and each of us, and we, at his request, in his presence and in the presence of each other, have hereunto subscribed our names as witnesses, this 15th day of August, 1968,

Name	Address
....	....
....	....
....	....

(NOTE: In many states, just two witnesses are required, but three are used as a precautionary measure.)

PART 3

Glossary
Of Terms

Administration. The conservation, management and settlement of an estate of a deceased person.

Administrator. A person or corporation appointed by a court to settle the estate of a person who has died intestate, i.e., without leaving a will. Fem. administratrix.

Administrator Cum Testamento Annexo, (administrator with the will annexed, abbreviated to administrator c.t.a.). A person or corporation commissioned by a court to settle the estate of a deceased person who named no executor in his will or when the person named in the will fails to qualify.

Administrator Cum Testamento Annexo de Bonis Non (abbreviated to administrator c.t.a.d.b.n.). One appointed by a court to complete the settlement of the estate.

Affinity. Relationship by marriage; as contrasted with consanguinity, which is relationship by blood.

Ancestor. One who precedes another in the line of inheritance. Originally, the term ancestor applied only to persons in the direct line of ascent (father, grandfather, or other progenitor), but the term now includes persons of collateral relationship such as uncles and aunts.

Ancillary. Auxiliary; such as ancillary administration and ancillary administrator.

Appreciation. Increase in value; opposite of depreciation.

Attest. To bear witness to; as, to attest a will.

Attestation Clause. The clause of a will containing the declaration of the act of witnessing; it follows the signature of the testator and usually begins, "Signed, sealed, published, and declared by the said . . .".

Attesting Witness. One who testifies that a document is authentic, as the attesting witness to a will. (See also subscribing witness.)

Authenticated Copy. A copy of a document certified by a court official to be a true and correct copy of the original.

Beneficiary. (1) One who is entitled to the profits of an estate. (2) The person for whose benefit a trust is created. (3) The person to whom the proceeds of an insurance policy are payable.

Bequest. A gift of personal property by will; a legacy.

Cestui Que Trust (pl., cestuis que trust.) The beneficiary of a trust.

Charitable Bequest. A gift of personal property to a charity by will.

Charitable Devise. A gift of real property to a charity by will.

Codicil. An amendment or supplement to a will. It should be executed with the same formalities as a will.

Collateral Heir. A person not in the direct line of the deceased; for example, a nephew or an uncle.

Consanguinity. Blood relationship. (See affinity.)

Contest of a Will. An attempt by court action to prevent the probate of a will.

Corpus (body.) The principal (capital) of an estate, as distinguished from the income.

Curtesy. The interest of a widower in the real property of his wife. Many states have abolished curtesy by statute.

Death Taxes. Taxes imposed on the transfer of property at death; a generic term covering estate taxes and inheritance taxes.

Decree. An order of a court of equity, to be distinguished from the judgment of a court of law.

Demise. (1) Death; decease. (2) To pass, by will or inheritance. (3) To lease, for life or a term of years.

Demonstrative Gift. A gift, by will, of a specified sum of money to be paid from a particular source; e.g. a gift of $1,000 payable from "my account at the First National Bank."

Depreciation. Decrease in value; opposite of appreciation.

Descendant. One who is descended lineally in a direct line from another, (child, grandchild, great-grandchild, etc.); the same as issue.

Descent. The transmission of an estate by inheritance.

Devise. A gift of real property by will. The person who receives the gift is the devisee.

Direct Heir. A person in the direct line of ascent or descent; as father, mother, son, daughter.

Dissent. To disagree. In probate law, a widow may dissent from her husband's will, and take the share provided for her by law. The will then governs the residue of the estate as though she predeceased him.

Distributee. A person to whom something is distributed.

Distribution. In law, the apportionment by a court of the personal property (or its proceeds) of one who died intestate among those entitled to receive the property according to the applicable statute of distribution; commonly used to refer to the distribution of property or payment of money to the heirs or beneficiaries of any estate.

Distributive Share. The share of a person in the distribution of an estate.

Domicile. The place where a person has his legal abode; the place of his permanent home; the place to which, whenever he is absent, he has the intention of returning. A person's domicile and his residence are not necessarily the same.

Donee. One who receives a gift.

Donor. One who gives.

Dower. The interest of a widow in the property of her husband. At common law a wife had a life estate in one-third of the real estate of her husband. In many states common law dower has been abolished or altered.

Election. The choice of an alternative. For example, the right of a widow to take the share of her deceased husband's estate to which she is entitled under the law, despite a contrary provision in the will.

Eleemosynary. Pertaining to charity; a charitable, non-profit institution is an eleemosynary institution.

Entail. To restrict an inheritance to a certain succession of heirs; e.g., to limit passage of the title to male heirs.

Entity. That which exists as separate and complete in itself. A corporation is an entity, separate and distinct from its stockholders. For many purposes, an estate is a separate entity.

Equitable Ownership. The beneficial interest of a person in property, the legal ownership of which is in another person. A beneficiary of a trust has an equitable interest in the trust property, while the trustee holds the legal title.

Escheat. The reversion of property to the state if there are no heirs or devisees.

Estate. (1) One's entire property. (2) Property left after death. (3) The right, title, or interest which a person has in any property; to be distinguished from the property itself, which is the subject matter of the interest.

Estate Tax. A tax imposed on a decedent's estate as such and not on the distributive shares of the estate or on the right to receive the shares; to be distinguished from an inheritance tax.

Executor. An individual or corporation nominated in a will and appointed by a court to settle the estate of the testator. Fem. executrix.

Exemplified Copy. A copy of a record or document certified by a proper official as required by law.

Failure of Issue. Failure, by nonexistence or death, of lineal descendants (children, grandchildren, and down the line.)

Fiduciary. (1) A position of trust or confidence. (2) A person who holds a position of trust. (3) A person charged with the duty of acting for the benefit of another party.

General Gift. A gift, by will, of personal property which is not a particular thing as distinguished from all others of the same kind.

Gift Causa Mortis. A gift of personal property made by a person in expectation of death, completed by actual delivery of the property, and effective only if the donor dies.

Gift Inter Vivos. A gift of property between living persons. To make such a gift effective, there must be actual delivery of the property during the lifetime of the donor.

Gift Tax. A tax imposed upon the value of a gift. The United States imposes the tax upon the donor, and the donee is liable only if the donor does not pay.

Guardian. An individual or corporation appointed by a court to care for the property or the person of a minor or an incompetent.

Guardian ad Litem. A person appointed by a court to represent a minor or an incompetent while a court action is pending.

Heir. A person who inherits from a deceased person.

Heir at Law. One who succeeds to a deceased person's estate by operation of law.

Holographic Will. A will entirely in the handwriting of the testator.

Income. The returns from property, such as rent, interest, and dividends; opposed to principal, capital, or corpus.

Incompetent. One who is legally incapable of managing his own affairs.

Incorporation by Reference. To make one document a part of another document by referring to it therein.

Indemnity Bond. An obligation in writing by which the signer, together with his surety or bondsman, guarantees to protect another against loss.

Infant. A person not of legal age.

Inheritance Tax. A tax on the right to receive property by inheritance; to be distinguished from an estate tax.

In Loco Parentis (in the place of a parent.) A phrase referring to a person who takes the place of a child's parent.

Intangible Property. Property which cannot be touched or realized with the senses, such as a legally enforceable right. Stocks, bonds and notes are called such.

Intestacy. The condition resulting from a person's dying without leaving a will.

Intestate. (adj.) Not having made a valid will. (Noun) A person who dies without leaving a valid will.

Issue. All persons who have descended from a common ancestor; offspring; progeny.

Joint Tenancy. The holding of property by two or more persons in such a manner that, upon the death of one joint owner, the survivor or survivors take the entire property.

Jurisdiction. The lawful right to exercise official authority; the right of a court to determine a particular cause; the territory over which such authority extends.

Kin. Persons of the same blood; persons with a common ancestor.

Kind. "Distribution in kind" means distribution of the property itself and not the cash equivalent.

Kindred. Persons related by blood.

Lapse. (Noun) A gift which fails, usually by reason of the death of the intended recipient during the testator's lifetime.

Laws of Descent and Distribution. Laws governing the descent of property, descent referring to real property and distribution to personal property.

Legacy. A gift of personal property by will; also called a bequest.

Letters of Administration. A certificate of authority to settle a particular estate issued to an administrator by the court.

Letters Testamentary. A certificate of authority to settle a particular estate issued to an executor by the court.

Life Estate. Either an estate for the life of the tenant or an estate for the life or lives of some person or persons.

Lineal Descendant. A person in the direct line of descent, as child or grandchild.

Minor. A person under legal age. (See also infant.)

Mixed Property. Property which has some of the attributes of both real property and personal property.

Natural Guardian. The parent of a minor.

Next of Kin. The person or persons in the nearest degree of blood relationship to the decedent.

Non Compos Mentis. Not of sound mind.

Nuncupative Will. An oral will made by a person on his deathbed or by one who is conscious of the possibility of impending death.

Pecuniary Legacy. A gift of money by will.

Pendente Lite. During the continuance of a court action.

Per Capita (by the head.) A term used in the distribution of property, contrasted with Per Stirpes, e.g., if testator gives to "my son and grandsons per capita", each take an equal share; but, if "per stirpes," the grandsons share their parent's share.

Personal Effects. Goods of a personal nature, such as clothes and jewelry.

Personal Property. All property other than real property.

Personal Representative. A general term applicable to both executor and administrator.

Personalty. Personal property.

Per Stirpes (by the stalk.) A term used in the distribution of property; distribution to persons as members of a family (per stirpes) and not as individuals (per capita). Two or more children of the same parent take per stirpes when together they take what the parent, if living, would take.

Posthumous Child. A child born after the father's death.

Power. Authority or right to do or to refrain from doing a particular act, as an executor's power of sale.

Power of Appointment. A right given to a person to dispose of property which he does not own.

Pretermitted Child. A child to whom a will leaves no share of the parent's estate without affirmative provision in the will showing an intention to omit.

Primary Beneficiary. A beneficiary entitled to receive the property or its benefits immediately.

Principal. The property of an estate other than the income from the property; the same as capital.

Probate Court. The court that has jurisdiction with respect to wills and intestacies and sometimes guardianships. Also called surrogate's court and orphan's court.

Probate of Will. Formal proof before the proper officer or court that the instrument offered is the last will of the decedent.

Residence. The place where one resides, whether temporarily or permanently.

Residuary Devise. A gift, by will, of the real property remaining after all specific devises have been made.

Residuary Estate. The property that remains after the testator has made provision out of his net estate for specific, demonstrative, and general gifts.

Rule Against Perpetuities. A rule of common law that makes void any estate or interest in property so limited that it will not take effect or vest within a period measured by a life or lives in being at the time of the creation of the estate plus twenty-one years. Many states have statutes with similar provisions.

Schedule of Distribution. A list showing the distributees of an estate, and their respective shares.

Secondary Beneficiary. A beneficiary whose interest in a trust is postponed or is subordinate to that of the primary beneficiary.

Settlement. The winding up and distribution of an estate by an executor or an administrator.

Specific Devise. A gift, by will, of a specific parcel of real property.

Specific Legacy. A gift, by will, of a specific article of personal property.

Spendthrift Clause. A provision in a will or trust instrument which limits the right of the beneficiary to dispose of his interest and the right of his creditors to reach it.

Statutes of Mortmain. A law restricting the giving or willing of property to ecclesiastical or charitable organizations.

Stock Power. A form of assignment executed by the owner of stock which contains an irrevocable appointment of an attorney to make the actual transfer on the books of the corporation.

Subscribing Witness. One who sees a document signed or hears the signature acknowledged by the signer and who signs his own name to the document, such as the subscribing witness to a will.

Succession. The fact of a person's becoming entitled to property of a deceased person, whether by operation of law or by taking under will.

Surcharge. (Noun) An amount which a fiduciary must make good because of some negligence or failure of duty on his part.

Tenancy by the Entirety. Tenancy by a husband and wife in such a manner that, except in concert with the other, neither husband nor wife has a disposable interest in the property during lifetime of the other. Upon the death of either, the property goes to the survivor. To be distinguished from joint tenancy and tenancy in common.

Tenancy in Common. The holding of property by two or more persons in such a manner that each has an undivided interest which, upon his death, passes as such to his heirs or devisees and not to the survivor. To be distinguished from joint tenancy and tenancy by the entirety.

Testamentary Capacity. Mental capacity to make a will.

Testamentary Guardian. A guardian named in the decedent's will.

Testamentary Trust. A trust established by the terms of a will.

Testate. Having made and left a valid will.

Testator. A man who has left a will at his death. Fem. testatrix.

Transfer Agent. An agent of a corporation to effect the transfer of the corporation's stock from one owner to another.

Trust Institution. A trust company, bank, or other corporation engaged in the trust business under authority of law.

Vest. To confer an immediate, fixed right of immediate or future possession and enjoyment of property.

Vested Interest. An immediate, fixed interest in real or personal property, although the right of possession and enjoyment may be postponed until some future date or until the happening of some event.

Waiver. The voluntary relinquishment of a right, privilege, or advantage .

Ward. A person who is under the protection of a guardian.

Widow's Allowance. The allowance to a widow for her immediate needs after her husband's death.

Will. A legally enforceable declaration of a person's wishes regarding the disposition of his property; the legal declaration of a man's intentions as to his estate after his death; a written instrument by which a person declares his desires as to the distribution of his property after death.